ACROSS WORLD FRONTIERS

The Misses Selby

Across World Frontiers

Thomas W. Lamont

New York

HARCOURT, BRACE AND COMPANY

INTRODUCTION

Father lived a full life and for many years he had had it in mind to write about it: about his boyhood in the Hudson Valley, his experiences here in America in business and banking, and abroad in international affairs. In his mind and from notes which he had kept, he had the material available from which he could have prepared a rather comprehensive history of the part that Wall Street and the Morgan firm played in domestic and foreign financing during the first four decades of this century. Or he could have written a carefully documented study of the Versailles Peace Conference and the subsequent history of German Reparations. But unfortunately the pressures of a busy life resulted in a constant postponement of the preparation of such books as he may have planned.

In the summer of 1943, Father became seriously ill. This forced him to relinquish some of his business and community activities; and in the latter part of that year he began writing some reminiscences of his youth. They were published in 1946 as *My Boyhood in a Parsonage*.

That book was Father at his best. It revealed his wisdom and his humor and his human traits.

Yet he still had it in mind to write at least one somewhat more serious volume and, despite his failing health, he started on the job in the summer of 1945. Partly dictating, partly writing longhand, he completed, at the end of 1947, the first drafts of the chapters contained in this book; but much still remained to be done when he died on February 2, 1948. With the exception of his trip to the Far East, the last twenty-five years of his crowded life had been unrecorded by him. His activities as a Morgan partner and the important role he played in American business remain largely unchronicled. Nor does this book tell his story of the post-war financing of Europe nor recount his part in the reparations conferences from which the so-called Dawes and Young plans evolved. This book, then, does not pretend to be a chronological narrative of my father's life as a whole.

Yet Father had put so much time and effort—so much of his wisdom and humor—into this unfinished work that it seemed a pity not to print it privately for circulation among family and friends. What better way than through his own well-told tale could future generations of descendants learn something of his solid achievements in the world of affairs? What better way to obtain a picture of the man's character and personality, to see him in those later years, beyond his boyhood in a parsonage, when he had attained full maturity and distinguished powers?

Accordingly, Father's original drafts were edited;

vi

and in this labor of pleasure and love my brother, Cor-liss, my mother, and I received the understanding advice of Miss Katherine McGuirk, my father's devoted secretary, as well as the skillful help of Miss Frances L. Van Schaick. Nothing of importance was eliminated, and those who know Father's turn of mind and phrase will recognize the story to be entirely his. The book was published privately, in the autumn of 1950.

So many friends enjoyed it so much that we finally came to the conclusion that regular publication was warranted; and this idea took definite form when Harcourt, Brace and Company decided to publish it.

We have chosen for the book the title *Across World Frontiers*, which is descriptive of the contents, and of Father's life and activities. More particularly it is descriptive, I think, of Father himself. First of all, he was devoted to his own country. But his was no narrow nationalistic patriotism. He loved his fellow man, whether he might be from New York, Kansas, China, or France. He saw clearly that, for the peace and well-being of America, Americans must understand and appreciate their neighbors across the seas as well as their neighbors on Main Street. He saw that only a peaceful world could insure a happy home anywhere. Everywhere between the lines of my father's narrative, implicit in his every activity, one can see his hope and prayer for his children's children and for all American youth that no frontiers would ever bind their minds or set limits upon their achievements.

THOMAS S. LAMONT

April, 1951

CONTENTS

I

The Early Years

1
VICTORIA REGINA

"The Queen, you know, is very fond of being Queen." This from the deep bass voice of Miss Lavinia Carbury, an Anthony Trollope spinster if there ever were one. If she did not hail from Barsetshire itself, it was surely some county close to the famous Trollope shire. She was spending the London season at the select pension and boarding house maintained by the Misses Bare and Bennett in Upper Baker Street.

This was some fifty years ago, in the summer of 1896, just when Conan Doyle, Sherlock Holmes, and Dr. Watson were making Upper Baker Street in Northwest London famous. I, then 25 years old, had had to go abroad on business — my first trip across the ocean. And, though I could ill afford it, I had taken my wife along. Hence our presence at the Bare & Bennett Inn, as we called it, with breakfast, luncheon, and dinner included. There were a dozen other boarders, all British, and mostly elderly women, spinsterish or widowish. They had come to London for the Season for the sole purpose of getting occasional glimpses of the Queen, old Victoria herself, her life and her era going gently out together.

3

Every pleasant afternoon — and July in London is rather apt to be sunny — those elderly dames took the bus down to Hyde Park Corner, going directly after luncheon and so being early enough to secure little iron seats on the margin of the Park driveway. If they had good luck, at a few minutes before four o'clock along came trotting a pair of rather diminutive horses, drawing in a low-cut landau the Queen. She always held a tiny sunshade and for the most part looked straight ahead. Now and then, however, she glanced to right and left to acknowledge the exceedingly dignified reception accorded her by the crowds which had gathered on either side of the drive. On the seat opposite the Queen, with her back to the driver, sat her lady-in-waiting, looking the part and exceedingly uncomfortable withal.

There had been that rather remote and somewhat romantic past when, just crowned, the young Queen had been exceedingly popular and always a figure for the social world to consider. But for twenty years following the death of the Prince Consort the Queen had kept herself apart, spending a prodigious amount of time in her Scottish fastness at Balmoral. With her Golden Jubilee in 1887, however, and her crowning as Empress of India (a title that she adored but that has now gone with the wind), she began once again to let herself be seen by the people. It was a public that, as I witnessed it, had an immeasurable respect and a great affection for the Queen.

My wife and I joined the throng several times, and each time got a close look at the aging monarch. I should say that on the whole she did not come up to her character quite as well as Helen Hayes did on the stage forty years later. But even so, the Queen's puffy little eyes, her pendulous cheeks, her rather grim look, and her figure which was not wrought with grace, were fairly faithful models for the later Helen Hayes. She had, too, something motherly about her, as Henry James noted at the time of her death five years later. "We all feel motherless today," he wrote to a friend. "We are to have no more of little mysterious Victoria, but instead fat vulgar dreadful Edward." At any rate, the original of the Queen, adequate or otherwise, was quite sufficient for the Bare & Bennett group which was always in raptures when it had been lucky enough to gaze upon the royal features.

Having come to London to spend their savings for this sole purpose, the Bare & Bennett boarders' sole topic at supper was talk of the Queen. "Did you see the Queen today?" ran around the long table. Or, "The Queen was looking a bit tired today." And then some elderly gossip from the other end — possibly the deep-voiced character from Trollope — would boom out: "Well, you know, the Prince of Wales, first gentleman of Europe that he is, is sometimes a great trial to the Queen." Then an awed silence would fall on the table, and great uneasiness that there had been any allusion to the sometimes gayer side of the Prince's life.

This to be sure was two or three years before the Prince of Wales (later Edward VII), met the beautiful Irish actress Mrs. Patrick Campbell, for the first time. "And where is your husband just now, Mrs. Campbell?"

5

inquired the Prince in that rather heavy Teutonic accent of his.

"He is with the army in South Africa," replied Mrs. Campbell with a saddened lilt in her tones.

"Oh, a very good place for a good man to be," responded the Prince with ready conviction. "Is he in the active fighting?"

"Yes, your Royal Highness, he is at the front."

"Better and better," responded the Prince, not recalling of course the biblical story of David and Uriah. "For a brave fellow like your husband that must be very satisfactory." And he promised himself the pleasure of waiting upon Mrs. Campbell herself the next day.

The old ladies at the Bare & Bennett never knew any of that, yet the mere allusion to the Prince had been the signal for the maîtresse d'hôtel, in such stentorian tones as to end all discussion, to announce the choice for dessert: "Suet Pudding, Gooseberry Tart, Genoese Pastry, or Trifle." And my conviction that it was a world of Anthony Trollope's that I was living in deepened as the talk ranged back and forth over the royal family — what a lovely person Princess Alice was, how devoted to her mother; how the Queen grieved over the death of her grandson, the Duke of Clarence, several years before; finally, what misfortune to have a grandson like that Kaiser Wilhelm II who only six years previously had taken over the ship of state from Prince Bismarck, and was now his own rather unruly and wilful pilot.

It was two years after this, in the summer of 1898, that I had my last glimpse of the old Queen. As I stood and watched her drive by that last summer, I wondered, as

6

I often had before, what was going on in the mind behind that sphinx-like but not unkindly visage. Did Victoria ever think of herself as encompassing and embodying an era, crowned as she was in 1837? According to the economists, it was 1848 before Britain's recovery from the effect of the Napoleonic wars was achieved. When Victoria was a girl, memory of those wars was as fresh to her parents and their generation as World War I is today to our middle-aged folk.

In the early years of her reign, the Duke of Wellington, that soul of integrity and common sense, was still a force for Victoria to reckon with. For her, Wordsworth, Shelley, Keats and Byron were still in the category of modern poets. For her, Alfred Tennyson, whom she ennobled, and Robert Southey and Robert Browning were contemporaries. Was she aware that her country, England, was the illustrious home of at least one great art — literature? How proud was she, I wondered, that her reign had produced that extraordinary group of great men of letters, names bewildering in their variety and richness: Sir Walter Scott, Dickens, Thackeray, Coleridge, Carlyle, Trollope, Meredith, Kingsley, Hardy, Macaulay, Froude, Arnold, Ruskin, and all the others? And did she feel pride in thinking of the scientists, inventors and explorers: Darwins, Bessemers, and David Livingstones?

Did Victoria know just what was meant by the Industrial Revolution of a half century before, or had she outlived the greatness of her era? For her the lights were growing dimmer, the memories of her great prime ministers less and less distinct — Disraeli, whose courtly

7

devotion she had adored; Gladstone, whose lighter reading were the Iliad and the Odyssey in the original, and
whom she respected, obeyed, and disliked.

Victoria was a far from great individual, yet all the
admiring common-folk of English people with whom I
mingled in the streets of London felt when she died that
a glory had departed from the earth, and they wondered
uneasily of the future. They seemed to sense that Victoria's mind to the end had still been filled with the
memory of her Prince Consort and of the love that she
bore him. For her there had never been any other man.
With his death the lights went out. Perhaps, too, to her
after all these years, as to most of us, there came:

> *. . . the dream*
> *Of lovelier life than this in some new earth,*
> *In the full summer of that unearthly gleam*
> *Which lights the spirit.*

Looking back, we can readily see now that the close
of the Victorian Era meant the finish of the tranquil
decades and a gradual change that forced us soon to
look out upon a more troubled world than that to which
we had been accustomed. Indeed, it was well enough
for me and my wife that there was stamped deep and
indelibly in our minds, at that time, a picture of the real
Europe — "that noble continent," as Mr. Churchill calls
it, "comprising on the whole the fairest and most cul-
tured regions of the earth, enjoying a temperate and
equable climate, the home of all the great parent races
of the Western World, the fountain of Christian faith
and Christian ethics."

8

2

EARLY TRIPS ABROAD

That first trip abroad in the spring and summer of 1896 is still more vivid in my memory than are any of the score or more subsequent ones that I made. So I get considerable pleasure in recalling, for the first time perhaps in many, many years, these fresh scenes and early impressions of a world that has largely vanished. The first trip abroad is always the best, and the years of youth and budding manhood in which I was revelling, taking in new sights and landmarks of history that I had been reading of all my life, still stand out in a rosy haze.

My wife and I embarked for Glasgow on a little old Anchor Line steamer, (only 3,000 tons burden), the *Anchoria*, rate for first-class passengers $65. Seawise it was a dreadful voyage. We bucked northeast storms all the way over, finally creeping into haven on the eleventh day in a tiny harbor in North Ireland where the natives came swarming out with fresh fish, milk and eggs — welcome provender for a tempest-tossed company that was working along as best it could on salt rations.

But I have seldom enjoyed a voyage more. It was an interesting ship's company with no idle rich, but rather

small-salaried college professors with their families. They
proved most congenial in every way. We could compare our travelling economies with almost the same satisfaction that we did the books we were reading.

On the twelfth day from New York we warped into
the quay at Glasgow where we spent a few hours view-
ing whatever was worth while in pictures or in objects
of historic interest. Then we sped on to beautiful Edin-
burg and put up at Waverley's Temperance Hotel on
Princes Street, which stands there to this day, I believe.
Perhaps we centered our sightseeing too much on the
scenes that Sir Walter Scott had long before furnished
us. But long haul, short haul, Sir Walter was not a bad
guide. We spent a day at Abbotsford—a good long day,
too. Thirty years later I went back there for an hour and
could hardly stand it. But on that first trip all my memories and thoughts of those days of chivalry that I had
absorbed so eagerly from the Waverley novels came
crowding back upon me.

Leaving Scotland (where in Argyllshire all my Lamont forbears for generations had lived and, in the
bloody seventeenth and eighteenth centuries, had fought
and died), we stopped for a couple of days at Chester.
I had always wanted to visit that ancient Roman camp
— castrum — to stroll on top of the ancient walls and
to get a bit of the spirit of Roman and Mediaeval England. And it was on that same trip that I acquired my
first set of Scott. Walking along the Roman Wall of
old Chester I espied a small and ancient bookshop below
me. For me its chief treasure was a Cadell & Whitaker
Edition of Scott (twenty-four volumes), little squat

books, type small but clear and legible, and the old steel engravings intact in each volume. I got it for a shilling a volume and still have it!

All London, when we arrived at the Misses Bare & Bennett, was ours for the asking. The English man of affairs had the happy faculty of knocking off work early. Accordingly the long summer afternoons found us journeying to Hampton Court or Richmond Park; one glorious day at the Henley Regatta; with hours left on many days to spend in the magnificent National Gallery in London.

It was there that the melancholy but pregnant voice of Charles Eliot Norton, of my years at Harvard College, came back to me with a real awakening of my memory, and made the pictures in the Renaissance group spring into life and beauty. The modern Tate Gallery and the Royal Academy exhibitions lacked the same romance, but their collections were always a delight for a young and eager wayfarer. The pre-Raphaelite school of painters had then, as we look back, rather passed its zenith. But for us Americans the work of Burne-Jones, Dante Gabriel Rossetti, William Morris, and the others was still fresh and lovely.

I shall always maintain that the only way to see London, at any rate in those days of mine a half century ago, was from the top of a bus — not a noisy, vulgar, motor vehicle, but one drawn by two sturdy horses (with an extra one hitched on for Ludgate Hill), and with a driver of the Dickensian era, cracking his whip and his jokes at the same time.

One route from the West to the East End of London

was by way of Oxford Street and so on through High Holborn and Holborn, running through Regent Circus and leaving at the right the delights of Regent and Bond Streets. The other route, even more alluring, was of course down Piccadilly, past the National Gallery, on into the Strand; jogging slowly up that entertaining thoroughfare, past the Christopher Wren churches, the Temple and the Inns of Court, on through Fleet Street and the great newspaper offices. So on to the City, the Mansion House (London's City Hall), the Royal Exchange, and to the Bank of England. Beyond that one glimpsed all those queer, twisty streets, lined with the shops of the merchants who dealt in tea and all sorts of goods from India, China, and the Far East.

It was American tourists, I suppose, that kept alive the old Cheshire Cheese, on an alley off Fleet Street. That small, ancient eating-house, reputed to have been frequented by Dr. Samuel Johnson, was almost always one of the early attractions for Americans. Consuming huge mutton chops for luncheon, we provincials were certain that we were sitting in the same cubicle and in the very seats that Dr. Samuel Johnson and his Boswell had occupied so many generations ago.

London's very vastness was overwhelming in those days — by far the largest city in the world. Our own metropolis seemed beside it almost a village. New York City fifty years ago consisted of Manhattan alone. Brooklyn was by itself the "City of Churches" and homes, and there were just the beginnings of a Bronx, of a Queens, and of a Richmond, which together in population now overshadow Manhattan.

In London, too, there seemed to a newcomer, un-sophisticated and fresh from the days of his youth, something that stirred the pulse and fired the imagination. Its streets, ancient and modern, and the density of its population, begat a sort of mystery — a conglomerate of tragedy, comedy, sweeping movements for reform, lords and ladies coming down the steps of the great houses in Grosvenor Square, the squalid and grimy homes of the dockers and their families in the far East End of London; music, laughter, lovely concerts, erudite and interesting lectures, all these on the one hand, and then close at hand, lurking in the alleyways, violence, murder, and sudden death. For me London was the most thrilling spot that I had ever known or could imagine existed. That was the London that I saw and felt a half century ago.

Our fortnight's holiday we had decided should be spent on the Continent, chiefly in Paris. We crossed the Channel in the smallest of craft and on tumbling seas, but reached the fairyland of Paris just at dusk, as the lights were beginning to spring up in all the squares and through the stately vistas of the Champs Elysees and so on to the Arc de Triomphe. L'Hôtel de l'Univers et du Portugal was our destination. Nobody had ever heard of it before, or since, in the fifty years that have elapsed since those Elysian days. Just why the Universe and Portugal, a very minor state, should have joined together for our delight I cannot tell. It had no rating in Baedeker. Yet its breakfast brioches and café au lait tasted divine. And no one of the many months since then that I have spent in the comfort of the Ritz or the

Meurice has ever afforded the complete satisfaction that Portugal and the Universe, situated in some obscure street en route between the Place de l'Opéra and Montmartre, provided for us.

In Paris, in these days before taxicabs had arrived, the means of locomotion for the well-to-do were the little one-horse open fiacres, with the cabbies shrieking oaths at their scraggly horses and indulging in the most ribald of side remarks for the benefit of the passenger. But I could seldom afford such luxury, and our means of locomotion was chiefly walking, and, for the longer distances, buses. For young people on a first visit nothing could be better. There was plenty of time for everything. The people were, just as you saw them in all the pictures, sitting on the sidewalks outside the restaurants and cafés, sipping their coffee or apéritifs, just as we knew they should. There were only peace in the world and happiness to look forward to. Those were bright, sunny days with the countryside outside Paris aglow under the fleecy French clouds and sky that hardly the native artists themselves have been able to do justice to.

As compared to London which has always seemed to me like a friend, Paris was more like a delightful acquaintance whose charm was unending, but with whom I should never wish to make my home. In those early days half a century ago the bookstalls lining the left bank of the Seine were even more alluring than they are today. The ancient fishermen casting their lines from bridge and bank were just as numerous. The whole region of la Rive Gauche, the Latin Quarter and all the smock-clad artists that lived their lives there, drew us to wander day after day through the narrow streets.

We never neglected the beauty and delight of the Louvre and its treasures. There for some inexplicable reason it was the heroic statue of the Victory of Samothrace that gave me the greatest thrill. And to this day I cannot look upon it without a quicker heart-beat, without gladness that over two thousand years ago lived those men of genius who could create images of beauty to move the hearts of men then and in all the centuries to follow; their field of inspiration in the Eastern Mediterranean, now the picture of devastation, desperate want, and civil war.

From Paris we journeyed by train to Belgium, rented bicycles, and pedalled slowly along the placid rivers, stopping for a day or two at Bruges and Ghent and working our way gradually through the Ardennes. Then we knew them as lovely, rather low-lying mountains; in these modern days we think of them in terms of the Battle of the Bulge and other bloody conflicts.

In those younger and more unsophisticated years of mine I made other trips abroad — no one naturally so vivid or so strong in the ineradicable impressions made upon me as that early first one. The others came: one in 1898, crossing the Atlantic just after war with Spain had broken out, one in 1901, another in 1902, again in 1905 (that one chiefly a brief golfing trip to St. Andrews in Scotland), a longer one in 1908 when I journeyed east as far as Vienna.

Looking back, I do not attempt to sort them all out.

I turn the kaleidoscope and at each angle a fresh and lovely memory, misty though it may be, turns up: Sitting at the bow of the little green canal boat from Rotterdam to Delft, the small donkeys — which furnished the only motor power available in those days — pulling doggedly at the tow-line, slowly enough to give us a wonderfully close and intimate study to right and left of the Dutch countryside and the life of the Dutch peasant.

Or perhaps (this, too, before the age of motors) we should be sitting gaily in a sturdy landau, the little coachman cracking his whip from time to time, and the two horses trotting steadily ahead of us up and down the slopes of the Dolomites. That was, I recall, a perfect trip, starting at Innsbruck and letting the leisurely days go by as we journeyed through the lovely mountains of the Tyrol. The clouds covered the summits that evening that we reached Lago di Misurina, on the frontier at the top of the pass, and with the morning's light gazed down the slopes of the Alps upon the red roofs of Cortina, and on into the valley of Italy. There awaited us a new world of sun shining on white walls, and a new thrill in the old world, as we looked at the glowing groups of primitives that crowded the galleries and churches.

And that delightful kaleidoscope of forty or fifty years ago, with all the useful economies or little hardships that we had to undergo to reach our end, never turns without disclosing some stately cathedral to bring added dignity and a touch of mysticism to the scene. In fact if, in later years, I had been asked what outward manifestations of Europe's beauty, dignity and history had most impressed me, I think I should have said its cathedrals, including those in the British Isles as well. Here were noble monuments of worship that had been designed and built with loving care in the far-distant centuries. So rare indeed was their Gothic architecture that for many generations after the builders had died and been forgotten people regarded these cathedrals as the work of supernatural beings.

There is no need to catalogue them in this brief reminiscence of mine. Of all the continental cathedrals, I was, like many others, drawn most to Chartres, as it rises out of the plain forty miles from Paris — its two towers forming a beautiful landmark for that region for all time. I wonder what the architects of that unsurpassable magnificence were thinking when they worked over the plans close to a thousand years ago. I only know that following that first visit, I have seldom been in Paris without journeying to that great monument with its gorgeous rose window.

Mr. Baedeker in a small red volume with fine print was always our *vade mecum*. And whenever we visited some point of particular interest, we fell into the habit of delving into the nearest available library and finding out what had befallen there in centuries long past. It might be that we were treading the ancient battlefields of Agincourt, Crécy, or Poitiers; or perhaps in Paris were gazing at the very spot in the Place de la Concorde where the tumbrils drove up to the guillotine that saw the end of Louis XVI and his Antoinette, whose prescription for the semi-starving populace was, if they

17

could not get bread, "Let them eat cake." And then that night, back in our little l'Univers et du Portugal, it might be, we would rush again through "A Tale of Two Cities" and see Sydney Carton as the tumbril slowly creaked and rumbled with him to his heroic fate. In those days it was still fun to read Charles Dickens.

As the crowded years went by and I visited London and in fact much of the outlying countryside of England with some frequency, I began to know my London fairly well. I recall one summer, shortly before the death of old Queen Victoria, I spent a couple of days taking a bus from the West End to explore the City of London. I wanted to look at the Bank of England, the Royal Exchange, and the Mansion House where the Lord Mayor held forth, and particularly to wander through the crooked streets where financial London had its abode, well to the east of St. Paul's Cathedral. Those narrow streets must still be crowded with ghosts, for through them in far-gone centuries roamed in turn Romans, Saxons, Normans — merchants, builders, men of the sea; the remains of ancient fortifications are still to be found in hidden nooks among the buildings.

I strolled along winding Old Broad Street, off Cheapside, and as I paused for a moment to ask a question from a passerby, he pointed out across the way the offices of the Morgan bank, with a rather narrow and certainly dingy enough frontage to be in line with the best traditions of the City of London. I had heard casually of the Morgan firm as occupying an important place in international banking: they had helped the French Government finance a part of the cash indemnity that it was forced to pay Germany after Germany's conquest of 1870-71, and after Kaiser Wilhelm I, as a special humiliation to France, had had himself crowned at Versailles as Emperor of the German Reich.

My thoughts might not have been quite so placid on that stroll through Old Broad Street if some wizard had been able to tell me that well within fifteen years I was to be associated with all three of the Morgan banks — in New York, London, and Paris. The London house was established by George Peabody under his own name, and he took in as his partner and successor a young American, Junius Spencer Morgan, father of the great J. Pierpont Morgan and grandfather of his son, J. P., the beloved associate of us all, who died only in 1943. Many legends about George Peabody have come down to those who have worked in the Morgan bank.

Mr. Peabody's repute rests now upon his splendid philanthropies: his establishment of the Peabody Donation Fund in London to which he gave a total of £500,000; his donation of $2,000,000 for the benefit of education in the South of our own country; the Peabody Museum of Natural History at Yale; the Peabody Museum of American Archaeology and Ethnology at Harvard; the Peabody Institute at Peabody and at Baltimore; the Peabody Museum at Salem; and so on. Mr. Peabody, who was graduated from Harvard College in 1823, was an American merchant who about 1830 had been induced to go into a British venture that turned out badly. But he was a persistent young man and decided to move to England to regain in business there what he had lost in his unfortunate previous venture.

19

He became a merchant-banker, dealing in bills of exchange, especially American, gradually expanded his international banking, and before many years had amassed a fortune.

Mr. Peabody was exceedingly careful in small economies, in regard to which various traditions had come down. One that the late Mr. Morgan told me was about Mr. Peabody and the penny bus. It seems that one morning when Mr. Peabody came to the office he had a very bad cold, and Mr. Morgan (this is J. S. Morgan, grandfather of my late chief) said to him: "Mr. Peabody, with that cold you ought not to stick here — you should go home and stay there"; and Mr. Peabody said, "I think I will, I feel very badly." Whereupon he put on his hat and took his umbrella, as it was raining, and went off. About twenty minutes later Mr. Morgan had to go to the Royal Exchange on some matter, and on the corner where the buses stopped (near where Mr. Peabody's statue now is) he saw Mr. Peabody standing in the rain. He at once said to him, "Why, Mr. Peabody, I thought you were going home." Mr. Peabody said in a very hoarse voice, "Well, I am, Morgan, but there's only been a tuppenny bus come along as yet and I am waiting for a penny one." And this within a year or two of his giving £100,000 in one sum for the poor of London!

That was about the time of our Civil War and business all over England was bad. The Federal blockade of the Southern ports cut off England's supply of raw cotton and the Lancashire spinners were without work. Their idleness affected many other industries, reaching up to London itself. Mr. Peabody became moved by the stories of the destitute in London and so gave his first £100,000 for relief. To the British this was a prodigious sum for an individual gift, and the news of it caused a great stir. Later on (her missive is dated March 28, 1866) Queen Victoria sent Mr. Peabody a letter dated at Windsor Castle, written in longhand and in the third person as is royal custom, always referring to herself as "the Queen." It was to thank him for his gift to the poor.

A copy of the letter, now a bit yellow with age, hangs in the Morgan offices in London today. The Queen's letter-paper has a heavy half-inch mourning band which she used throughout the whole forty years of her life after the death of the Prince Consort in 1861. The passage below indicates the extravagance of her gratitude, incidentally alluding as she does to "the wants of the poorer class of her subjects," a phrase which the British King and Queen of today might hesitate to use.

The Queen stated "how deeply she appreciates the noble act of more than princely munificence by which he has sought to relieve the wants of the poorer class of her subjects residing in London. It is an act as the Queen believes wholly without parallel, and which will carry its best reward in the consciousness of having contributed so largely to the assistance of those who can little help themselves. The Queen would not, however, have been satisfied without giving Mr. Peabody some public mark of her sense of his munificence."

One can, then, perhaps gain from these brief memories an inkling of the deep impress which these early foreign trips had upon me, making me feel that we Americans were linked to those countries of Western

Europe in ways that must never be broken.

The Europe that I was traversing as a young man was the Europe to which the world owes its civilization, the Western Europe that Charlemagne ruled as the Holy Roman Empire; that great area where Christianity was established once and for all; that vast plain, bordered by the Atlantic Ocean, that had lived its hard life through the Dark Ages, to come out triumphantly in the glories of the Renaissance; a region differing vastly in thought, religion, and life from that of Eastern Europe.

Today, as we gaze at the confusion and misery of a good part of that world, brought about directly by the evil philosophy and the greed for conquest of the Germans, we are apt to forget what we owe to Western Europe. We do not grasp the fact that every effort that we make to restore it, will repay us a thousand-fold in the benefits that we ourselves on this side of the Atlantic shall gain.

In the years of which I have been writing, when I was making my occasional trips to Europe, the part that America was to play in world affairs was not an urgent issue and did not become so until the end of our war with Spain. Then began the debate as to whether we should take up the white man's burden in Puerto Rico, and more especially of course, in the Philippines. The decision to make them both our wards was reached in the United States Senate only after long and earnest debate about the possible headaches involved for us in an affirmative course.

After that the matter of American expansion in foreign affairs seemed rather to die down for a dozen years, or until every question was thrown wide open by the outbreak of World War I in July, 1914. For three-quarters of a century we had rested content with the Monroe Doctrine which could never have been adopted or made effective had it not had Britain's warm support. For decades, as we all know well enough, it was the British fleet that had guarded the Seven Seas, and in fact made the Monroe Doctrine, so far as South America was concerned, a living thing. Prime Minister Canning drew up the Doctrine and submitted it to President Monroe for his approval and announcement. It was a fine piece of statesmanship and one of the great moves that served to save us from world wars during the last eighty years of the nineteenth century.

Even though I did not realize it at the time of which I am writing, the closing years of the nineteenth century, my feeling for the British people must have been steadily forming during those early visits of mine to the British Isles. Thus it did not require Dunkirk and the German blitz of 1940 to convince me that in face of danger to their country the British people were absolutely dauntless; that they were never dismayed by disaster; that they had long before set for us the pattern of individual and civil liberty, of change by evolution rather than revolution.

I remember the June morning of 1940 after France had fallen, a rather important individual strolled into the Morgan offices and, standing between Mr. J. P. Morgan's desk and my own, remarked sadly: "Well, France has fallen to the enemy. It will be England's turn next."

23

Mr. Morgan leapt to his feet fiercely, and declared almost violently: "England defeated! England conquered! Never, I tell you, never will that come about — never, never, never!" And Mr. Morgan, who knew the British people through and through, was right.

I am not at all sure that England did not even more clearly show the liberty-loving principles that she held dear for herself and for the world when in September, 1939, the people of that land, shrinking as they did from war, yet insisted that their Government should fulfill its pledge to Poland, and throw down the gauntlet against Hitler's ceaseless extension of tyranny — even though destruction itself might threaten their beloved island. Down through all time it will be Britain's glory that she did not wait to be directly attacked. And we in the United States may be proud that from that same stock came many of the early settlers who established the straggling colonies that became the American nation.

FIRST YEARS OUT OF COLLEGE

Going back to my own modest undertakings: after graduating from Harvard College in 1892, and finishing my active newspaper work in 1894, I was an executive in a commercial enterprise for a decade, then went into finance, drawn by my partner and friend, Henry P. Davison, into the group that was organizing the Bankers Trust Company. In that nine- or ten-year interval of active business prior to the organization of the Bankers Trust Company in 1903, my life in affairs was full of experience, mostly unhappy, but all of value to me.

When I finished Harvard, I found myself the Monday after graduation at the offices of the old *New York Tribune* on Park Row. The City Editor, Arthur F. Bowers, a Brown University man, brilliant but explosive at times, shook hands and gave me a place on the staff of reporters. My first week's pay was $5, but it went up after that, and in all fairness one must recall that the country was in the midst of the so-called Cleveland depression—due to causes with which President Cleveland had nothing to do and indeed which he fought manfully, against great odds, to remove. That is another story: the part that Government, not Big Business, played in precipitating the economic slump.

Newspaper offices in the days of which I speak, the early '90s, seemed far more like bedlam than they do today, and they were largely lacking in our present mechanical facilities, then absent from ordinary life. I am speaking, for example, of the time of the Presidential campaign of 1892 — Cleveland and Stevenson (who were elected) against the then Republican President Benjamin Harrison (whose grandfather had been President forty years before) and, for Vice President, Whitelaw Reid, the publisher of the *New York Tribune*.

One would of course expect special facilities for the gathering and transmission of news, particularly in this campaign. But beyond an occasional extra correspondent at Washington (the *Tribune* had only one) and a special letter every now and then from some important centre like Chicago, there was not very much extra effort until perhaps just a fortnight or so before election day when the powers that be were galvanized into action.

What was true of the *Tribune* was true of all the New York press with the exception, I should say, of Joseph Pulitzer's *New York World* which was straining every nerve to maintain its preeminent rank in circulation, as against competition from William Randolph Hearst's *Journal* which was about to take the field in a big way. These two offices were ahead of all the others in equipping their people with time-saving facilities such as, for example, typewriters for reporters.

The most striking lack from our modern-day point

26

of view was the telephone service. Believe it or not, there was in the editorial offices of the *Tribune* only one telephone, with no extensions and, of course, no switchboard or operator. I can see that telephone now attached to the wall just back of the Night City Editor's desk. About half after nine o'clock each evening but Sunday, the Managing Editor, Donald Nicholson, trotted around to the various departments and made notes of the chief items in the next day's news. Then he would come into the City Room and use the one telephone to reach Mr. Reid at Ophir Hall in Westchester, tell him what was going on, and get his instructions. Nicholson was an old Scotsman with lovely brown eyes and white hair, the gentlest man in the world, whose newspaper training had been confined to the interesting job of secretary to Mr. Whitelaw Reid.

From time to time a little slip from Nicholson might give us brief hints as to the handling of news. If election day, national or local, were approaching, "D. N." might send us a casual memorandum to the effect that for the moment there was perhaps no particular point in slamming the Tammany Hall leaders by name. It was they that had the allocation among the local press of the valuable election advertising that printed the addresses of the thousands of polling booths throughout the city. In those very hard times of 1892-93 revenues as well as economies were essential. As for the latter, I recall one week when orders had come down from on high that by hook or crook the entire weekly expense, including payroll, of the City Department, must be cut from $1,100 to $800 per week!

Sunday had its particular hardship, because power for the elevators was always shut off. The editorial offices were on the ninth floor. This meant that the entire editorial staff, many of them middle-aged men, had to climb, as best they could, at least once and generally twice a day up those eight long flights.

Sunday was, quite contrary to my early training, a day especially hard for me, for I had taken on the extra job of working with the financial editor in a grim basement office in Wall Street, to make up the tables of railroad earnings for the Monday paper. Very good training for me undoubtedly, and one that came in handy when I went into Wall Street banking a decade later. But it was a dog's job and I had no competition when I volunteered for it. The other reporters in the office used to poke fun at me, saying that I was always trying to learn the job of the man just ahead of me. This was more or less true. I did not want that man's job, but when it became vacant through his promotion I wanted to be sure I could qualify for it.

This time of which I am speaking now was when I had been promoted from the reporter's job to become one of the assistant night city editors, editing and correcting "copy" — that is, the stories of the day's happenings that the reporters wrote, passing them along to the City Editor's desk from 5 P.M. to 1 A.M. This job kept me at work later at night, but it gave me an excellent view of the whole business of gathering and presenting the news; and as time went on the responsibility centering around my own desk in handling of emergency news late at night became steadily greater.

This gave me just the experience in executive work that I wanted. Yet at the end of two years which were both wearing and entertaining, and sometimes thrilling, I could see little ahead in the newspaper field for years to come, except a rather hard grind, with compensation inadequate for a young man that wanted to get on in the world, specifically to marry and raise a family. So in August, 1894, I gave notice of my intention to leave the *Tribune*. They were all very charming, and Mr. Bowers gave me a letter of commendation most generous in its expressions.

I had received an offer to join the staff of a concern called Cushman Bros. To one completely ignorant of business it seemed attractive, though to one of normal experience it would have looked dubious. The only two difficulties about the business were, as they later developed: one, it was losing money steadily and rather heavily; two, its capital was totally inadequate for the type of business and the amount of overhead (that is, salaries of the top officers) that it was trying to swing.

Most young men entering affairs would have sense enough to inquire whether the small business they were joining was making or losing money. But I, being of a trusting nature, failed to ask whether the particular enterprise I was joining was operating in the black or in the red. Further, when I was told that it was essential to my position as secretary to the corporation that I should invest at least $5,000 in its shares, I assumed, incorrectly as it turned out, that I was adding that amount to the company's working capital, whereas I was buying stock from one of the senior officers who wanted to get rid of it. If I had not lacked even ordinary common sense I should have been saved endless anxiety, and even anguish, for my precious $5,000 that I put in was made available only by my insuring my life, and borrowing the money from a kind and aging relative, and by pledging the insurance policy, the annual premium on which was 15% of my salary.

My own idea of the nature of the business I was entering on that bright September day in 1894 was, I will confess, pretty hazy. I found myself in a comfortable office in Hudson Street on the lower west side. As secretary of the company I had a small roll-top desk assigned to me and had put before me the job of writing advertisements for a new brand of oatmeal. This work was not too uncongenial. But in devoting my recent training in English composition under Harvard's distinguished Barrett Wendell, LeBaron Briggs and others, to extolling the virtues of a particular brand of cereal, I must admit I felt somewhat fallen in my own esteem.

The business of our company was to act as "Agents for Manufacturers." In those simple days many out-of-town producers of branded food products were anxious to capture the New York market but were too small to maintain there a selling staff of their own. Our company, with a staff of ten or twelve active salesmen, could offer equal facilities to a half dozen or more manufacturers, and with good luck gain a firm foothold for their products in the metropolis. For our work we charged the producers a fixed fee plus a small commission on the sales that we made. In theory the idea sounded all right, but it did not work very well in practice, especially if general business were bad. And the middle and late nineties proved to be dark days of increasing trade losses for our affairs as well as for many others.

There was one redeeming feature of the business that was of immeasurable interest and advantage to me. I took upon myself to be the company's foreign courier, so to speak, to go abroad whenever a chance offered that a sound European manufacturer might be interested to appoint us to represent his firm in America. There seemed to be a somewhat better outlook abroad for such arrangements than at home. It was these trips which afforded me so much pleasure in 1896 and 1898.

In the summer of 1898, after I had spent four discouraging years as the junior officer of the company where I had cast my lot, the business was continuing its downward course. So it was that, after showing superb patience, the chief creditor at that time, an individual of very generous impulse who seemed to think that what money was for was to be lent without interest or without security, very reasonably decided that drastic changes must be made or the business closed up. I at once offered to withdraw, for the city editorship of the *New York Evening Post* had been offered to me. Scribner's had also offered me a job, but Mr. Charles Scribner, who was most cordial, doubted — and quite properly, without question — that my services were worth what I brashly thought they were.

As things turned out, I remained in the business. To my surprise I was told by the generous creditor of our little company that I was to reorganize and manage it by myself. Thus in 1898 I with my brother-in-law, Charles

Corliss, founded the business of Lamont, Corliss & Co. It had gradually become clear to me, as I worked through the dismal and unprofitable previous four years, that the set-up of the business was all wrong. For if ever we made an outstanding success in establishing a manufacturer's brand of goods, then he would be likely to dispense with our company as agents and carry on by himself. It was clear that to have a permanent business, we must ourselves become manufacturers on our own account, even though at the start on a small scale; and thus own and permanently control our own affairs and our efforts.

To this end I had great good luck. I hit upon two specialties that, from small beginnings, we were able to build up to something highly substantial. For five years it was a narrow squeak, but after that we were able to go ahead on a sound, compact basis and were finally able to pay off in full the old creditors. From that time on the business became an outstanding success, which it is to this day.

4

I BECOME A BANKER

In 1903, five years after the good turn in my business fortunes that came late in 1898 and the success that followed it, my good luck turned up again. A group of active young bankers, executive officers of national banks, had been conferring for months, under the leadership of the brilliant Henry P. Davison (later my immediate predecessor at J. P. Morgan & Co. and for years before and after that my intimate friend). Their idea was that with others among the younger bankers they should organize and have shares in a trust company whose soundness would appeal to the public, its directorate being made up wholly of bankers. They could direct to such an institution so-called trust business that, under the existing laws, the banks of which they were active officers were not permitted to handle. To make a long story short, the Bankers Trust Company was organized and launched on March 30, 1903, with a strong and active directorate of younger men outstanding in the banking world. The shares of the company were so popular that on the day they were issued they sold at $300 per share, just double the subscription price.

The astonishing success of the new institution was attributed largely to the attention bestowed upon it by its young directorate and by its eager though limited staff of officers of which I became one. Every year for ten years after the establishment of the Company in 1903, the Executive Committee of which I was secretary met every Thursday night for dinner in town at 6:30 and worked over the affairs of the institution until about 10:30 p.m. Those meetings, as I can bear witness, and the constantly fresh leads for trust business for the company that were aroused by the talk back and forth, were what established the firmness and speedy growth of the Bankers Trust Company in the first years of its existence. When it was nine years old it had become so important in the New York banking group that it erected its present dignified home at Wall and Nassau Streets.

The stately pinnacle of the Bankers Trust Building, soaring into the sky above its twenty-five stories, is almost an exact replica of the beautiful, classic tomb at Halicarnassus. But the building, with all that it stands for in sound banking and business, is, it must always be said, a monument to Henry P. Davison.

Just how did I have the good fortune to alight in the midst of these young Medici, these Fuggers, these Fortunatuses, as I regarded them? Although I had long been a friend of Davison, I had had absolutely no business with him before he began to organize the Bankers Trust Company, although once or twice he asked me how I had been lucky enough to succeed in the old bankrupt mercantile business that had burdened my life. But George Case, the lawyer, of White & Case, has long ago

34

told for both our families the story of how I happened to be made secretary and treasurer of the Bankers Trust at its very organization, — I who knew nothing of banking save from the outside looking in.

Case says that Davison and he were returning to Englewood, where we all lived, one icy February night about ten o'clock, on one of those Northern Railroad of New Jersey suburban trains which sneak up to Englewood behind the Palisades, after all well-regulated commuters had long been safely in the bosoms of their families. Davison and Case had been staying in town for dinner with the other men interested in the organization of the Bankers Trust Company, and they had been discussing this very question of executive officers. I, too, as it so happened, had been kept in town by my business and was going home that evening on the same train.

Case says that Davison had just been saying: "We have enough banking talent on our official staff, but where in the world can we get that plain business man that we want?" Just then I came strolling up the aisle. Davison gave Case a poke. "There's the man!" he said, and next morning he sent for me to make the proposal.

"I believe," said he to me, "that you are the man for our secretary and treasurer."

"But," I responded, "I don't know the first thing about banking. All my brief business life I have been borrowing money — not lending it."

"Fine!" retorted Davison, "that's just why we want you. A fearless borrower like you ought to make a prudent lender."

And that was how I happened to become a banker.

I did not know then, nor do I know to this day, the techniques of banking. I was shoved up with the other officers on the bridge. Perhaps that was the wrong way to become a banker, but it was the only way for me.

After six active and happy years with the Bankers Trust Company, urged on to greater effort by promotion to a vice presidency and directorship, I was called to a vice presidency of the First National Bank, "old Fort Sherman," because it had been so staunch for resuming specie payments under Secretary of the Treasury Sherman in 1879. My entry into the First National was just at the end of the money panic of 1907 which, because of our antiquated Federal banking laws, affected the whole country and was most difficult to control. Congress had been so negligent that it had afforded little protection to our banking situation since President Jackson had stupidly, on political grounds, thrown the Bank of the United States out the window sixty years before.

In New York City the money panic centered on several institutions that for years had been loosely managed. They were trust companies that had no place in the New York Clearing House and so when trouble came had no shelter to turn to. The panic took the form of runs by depositors on several institutions in question — the Knickerbocker and the Trust Company of America being the chief ones. There was terrific excitement. J. P. Morgan, the elder, came hurrying home from an Episcopal Convention at Richmond, Virginia, and at once formed a rescue party headed by himself, James Stillman of the National City Bank, and George F. Baker of the First National Bank.

After about ten days of turmoil and effort the situation, with the crisis hourly becoming more acute, culminated in an evening conference at Mr. Morgan's library in 36th Street where most of the leading bankers were summoned. This was in October, 1907. On no test could I be rated as a leading banker, but I was taken along as an experienced errand boy.

I did not arrive at the meeting until late at night. Two different groups of bankers were there: the commercial bankers who felt they had already met their worst difficulties were in the East Room, and the rather distraught Trust Company presidents in the gorgeous West Room. The total gathering constituted of course the famous all-night meeting that has become one of the traditions of the late J. Pierpont Morgan's career.

A more incongruous meeting place for anxious bankers could hardly be imagined. In one room were lofty, magnificent, tapestries hanging on the walls, rare Bibles and illuminated manuscripts of the Middle Ages filling the cases; in another, that collection of the Early Renaissance masters—Castagno, Ghirlandaio, Perugino, to mention only a few — the huge open fire, the door just ajar to the holy of holies where the original manuscripts were guarded. An anxious throng of bankers, too uneasy to sit down or converse at ease, paced up and down the lofty chambers and through the lovely marble hall.

President Edward King of the Union Trust Company had by common consent been selected as the leader or dean of the trust company presidents. After hours of conference and the display of all the figures by the accountants, Mr. Morgan pointed out to Mr. King, as to his fellow executives, that action must be taken, that a fresh loan of $25,000,000 must be made to save the Trust Company of America or the walls of the other edifices might come crumbling about their ears. He declared that, while he could not vouch for the figures, the experts (Benjamin Strong and his associates) had just reported that the Trust Company was solvent and that, therefore, no loss ought to result from this loan (as the event proved to be the case); and that as the Clearing House banks (at that time the trust companies were not, as I say, members of the Clearing House) were looking after the general situation, it necessarily devolved on the trust companies to look after their own, so to speak.

Yet the trust company presidents were reluctant to act. They felt that in the absence of their directors they had no authority to commit their institutions. They questioned whether their first duty was not to conserve all their assets for the storm which, despite everything, might burst upon them. Mr. Morgan understood well enough their situation. Inwardly he sympathized with them. But he had a task to accomplish. The situation must not get further out of hand. It had to be saved. Briefly he pointed out the chief factors in the situation. He said he was satisfied that if each trust company president present signed for an amount computed fairly on the basis of his company's resources, etc., the several boards of directors would surely ratify the action.

By this time Mr. Lewis Cass Ledyard, Judge Morgan J. O'Brien and other lawyers had agreed upon the form of a simple subscription blank to make up the total loan of $25,000,000. One of them read it aloud to the assembled bankers. Then they laid it on the table. Mr. Morgan waved his hand invitingly towards the paper. "There you are, gentlemen," he said.

The bankers shifted from one foot to another, but no one stepped forward. Mr. Morgan waited a few moments. Then he put his hand on the shoulder of his friend, Edward King, and gently urged him forward. "There's the place, King," he said kindly, but firmly, "and here's the pen," placing a handsome gold pen in Mr. King's fingers. Mr. King signed. The ice was broken. They all signed. Mr. King had been neither more nor less hesitant than the others. It had simply fallen to his lot to lead off when the crucial moment came.

That famous all-night conference at Mr. Morgan's Library, where the banks and trust companies came forward with enough money to meet the desperate situation, restored confidence in New York City that spread throughout the country. So the panic died down. Congress, however, had properly become so concerned that it belatedly appointed a joint Congressional Committee under the chairmanship of Senator Aldrich of Rhode Island to investigate the country's whole banking system, and to go abroad and study the systems in effect there where the banking communities were not plagued with occasional currency panics like our own. Meanwhile Mr. Morgan, having largely through his initiative and leadership saved his country from an almost calamitous financial situation, retired to Bar Harbor to finish his interrupted holiday.

I had only glimpses of Mr. Morgan in the next two years. He was a director of the First National Bank, on the board of which Mr. Baker had made me a director, in addition to my vice presidency. Mr. Morgan and all the others, including James J. Hill, the great builder of the Great Northern Railway, one of the titans of that period, attended the meetings regularly. These meetings at the First National were of immense interest to me because of the men who took part in them. Mr. Morgan was always cordial but took no particular notice of me.

One morning in late October of 1910 I received a telephone message that the senior Mr. Morgan would like to see me at his office. So I walked down to No. 23 Wall Street. The guards showed me through the double doors into the back offices. This, mind you, was the old Drexel Building, erected years before, only a few stories high, with a mansard roof, all in the period when the firm was styled Drexel, Morgan & Co.

As I entered the rear room the senior Mr. Morgan spoke to me from his desk. "Come over by me," he said, wishing me a good morning. Then he said abruptly, "Lamont, I want you to come down here as a partner on January 1st next."

I was astonished beyond words.

"But what can I do for you that is worth while?" I finally stammered out. "Oh, you'll find plenty to keep you busy," Mr. Morgan responded, "just do whatever you see before you that needs to be done," and rather seemed to think the interview at an end.

"Oh, wait," he said, "you'll come of course, won't you?"

40

"Mr. Morgan," I replied, "I am pleased beyond words that you should want me. But Mr. Baker has been exceedingly kind and generous with me. I can say nothing to you until I have talked with Mr. Baker."

"Oh, that's all right," said Mr. Morgan. "I have already talked with him of course." And he rather seemed to think that had settled the matter.

"Nevertheless, I must talk first with Mr. Baker, Mr. Morgan," I said.

"Oh, yes, quite all right," he responded. "Hope to see you here the first of the year."

Then, not given to the practice of uttering moral sentiments aloud, he turned and twisted in his seat a moment. "You know, Lamont," he said, "I want my business done up there," holding his hand high over his head, "not down there," pointing to the floor.

And that was how I entered the Morgan bank.

THE HOUSE OF MORGAN

Two or three bankers were awaiting the arrival of some partner when, on that second day of January, 1911, I came down early, to sit for the first time at a rather shabby, roll-top desk in the Morgan offices. The delegation explained that they headed two smallish uptown institutions, the Twelfth Ward and the Nineteenth Ward Banks that badly needed help. They had no possible claim on the Morgan firm, they said, but had nowhere else to go. This was the formula that I was destined to hear many times in the succeeding years.

As they unfolded their story, it appeared that they had become involved with the affairs of the newly created Carnegie Trust Company, which, we had heard, was already in hot water. Mr. Andrew Carnegie, who was then alive, had consented to let a new trust company bear his name, without making sufficient inquiries as to the character of the people responsible for the organization of it. Mr. Leslie Shaw, formerly Secretary of the Treasury, was in the same way gullible enough to allow himself to be named president of the new institution. It had a short and discreditable life.

The connection of the two banks with the Carnegie had become known, and runs had begun on the two uptown institutions. They had only about $6,000,000 of deposits between them, but they had thirty thousand depositors. The small banks had unhappily taken participation in some of the Carnegie Trust Company's undesirable operations, and the two uptown institutions would, unless the runs were halted by fresh backing, have to close their doors. That was their story!

We looked over their statements and it was evident that while, with time and skill, their affairs might possibly be worked out, they were presently insolvent. We could not see how we could possibly be expected to come to the rescue. To this statement the bank officials did not demur; however, we suggested that before they depart we get in touch with the elder Mr. Morgan at his Library uptown.

We told Mr. Morgan this story over the telephone. He asked only one question. That was concerning the character of the deposits in the two banks. The waiting group replied to our inquiry that their depositors were "mostly small East Side tradesfolk, working people, dressmakers and the like, who had deposited their all with the banks."

"Well," said Mr. Morgan over the telephone, "some way must be found to help these poor people. We cannot let them lose all they have in the world. Suppose at the worst we were to guarantee the payment of these $6,000,000 of deposits. Certainly our firm could not lose more than that amount."

Then Mr. Morgan added: "But we want no interest

43

in, or responsibility for, the conduct of those two banks."
I mention this because, in accordance with the practice
of certain newspapers — few, I am glad to say — head-
lines shortly appeared: "Morgan Grabs Two More
Banks."

I was startled at Mr. Morgan's sweeping suggestion
of guarantee, and not too happy at the idea of com-
memorating my first day of business under his leadership
by undertaking a handsome loss for my own account.
Yet, of course, in accordance with Mr. Morgan's suggestion, we set out, Harry Davison leading, to see what
could be done. We gave sufficient assurance to the State
Superintendent of Banks to justify him in using our
name in a public statement that indicated our support
for the banks. That, with an advance the Morgan firm
made of $700,000, was sufficient to stop the runs. Mean-
while other uptown bankers, interested to add to their
business, had come forward and arranged under certain
conditions to take over the beleaguered institutions.
When, months later, the final clean-up came, our firm
got off with a loss of about $180,000, plus days and
nights of work and consultation, and little thanks from
any quarter. The usual attitude seemed to be that our
firm existed for the purpose of saving lost banking
souls.

The year that I entered the Morgan firm and the
one following it witnessed the tearing down of the old
brownstone banking house on "the Corner," built in the
'70s, and the construction of our present offices upon
the same site. For the time being we had to occupy
cramped quarters in the old Mills Building at No. 15

Broad Street. In the midst of the building melee there was no seclusion or quiet for Mr. Morgan. So he maintained his headquarters in the West Room of the lovely Morgan Library in 36th Street, that room which I have already described.

Consequently, we partners made it a practice, one or two at a time, to stop off at the Library to consult with Mr. Morgan on matters of importance to the firm. He had of course extraordinary acumen in sizing up any given situation, and in outlining what our attitude towards it might well be. Far more often than otherwise he approved in a word the recommendations that we laid before him. From those not infrequent discussions, however, it was possible for a new partner like myself, just turned forty years of age, to discern the simple business philosophy which our Senior had unconsciously formulated over the years.

Mr. Morgan believed in people. He expected them to believe in one another, and to believe in him. Any rare instance of bad faith that came to his attention, even after over fifty years of business with all sorts and conditions of men, caused him surprise, dismay and distress. Further, I never recall an instance when, if we laid before him a new proposition, he asked first as to the possible profit in it. His first question was always as to its bearing upon the whole situation, whether beneficial or not. He was not interested in little matters, conducted or proposed by little men. Pericles in his great funeral oration says, "Wealth to us is not mere material for vainglory, but an opportunity for achievement." So it was with J. Pierpont Morgan.

Those less than three years of association with Mr. Morgan, thirty-five years or more ago, still stand out in my memory as a kind of golden age of chivalry in affairs. Nor is that memory kindled because of any great profit accruing to me. I well remember that in my first year the firm did badly, which for me meant no income but a heavy loss. I wondered just a bit whether I had got into an abode for eleemosynary projects. At any rate, however, I became steadily more impressed with the extent to which my senior partner, his son, and the firm generally, enjoyed the confidence of the community, in the integrity of their motives and the straightforwardness of their dealings.

I have sometimes seen the elder Mr. Morgan described as brusque and overbearing in his personal relations. Nothing could be further from the truth. He, like his son after him, had a most engaging personality, infinite kindness both in purpose and in manner. I well remember one of the first conversations I had with him after he had invited me to become a partner. I told him with considerable hesitation that Morgan partners had sometimes had the repute of working themselves to death. I wanted to be so bold as to say that I had no such intent and would like to feel free, except in times of emergency, to take each year total time off of three months. I felt that I was being guilty of the most awful effrontery.

"Why, of course," said Mr. Morgan, "take off as much time as you like. That is entirely in your hands."

Then he went on characteristically to say: "Lamont, why don't you go to Egypt this coming winter with your family? Just charter a dahabeah at Cairo and spend a few weeks on the Nile. It is a beautiful trip. You will want to go again and again."

I thanked Mr. Morgan warmly but explained that I had four young children, and this attractive suggestion was for me hardly practicable.

"Nonsense," said Mr. Morgan, "take along a couple of nurses, and you will be all right. That was what I did with my children when they were young."

It was seventeen years later that my wife and I were able to take Mr. Morgan's advice, and make the memorable trip up the Nile.

Nothing in the slightest degree adequate or even accurate has ever been written regarding Mr. J. Pierpont Morgan's long career in affairs (roughly from 1860 until his death in 1913) and the constructive deeds that he accomplished.* The volume written by his son-in-law, the late Herbert L. Satterlee, contains a delightful account of his earlier days. There have been alleged biographies, under lurid titles — *Morgan the Magnificent*, for example, and others. But the author of not a single one of these had ever met Mr. Morgan or had even, so far as I can learn, talked with any of Mr. Morgan's associates or friends. The consequence has been that such portions of the public as have read any of these sketches have gained a completely erroneous impression of Mr. Morgan, attributing to him untold wealth, vast powers that he was constantly seeking to increase in the banking and industrial fields; picturing him as an

---

* *Editor's Note* — Since this was written Frederick Lewis Allen has published a first-rate biography entitled *The Great Pierpont Morgan*, Harpers, 1949. Mr. Lamont himself has given some account of J. Pierpont Morgan and the Morgan firm in his *Henry P. Davison: The Record of a Useful Life*, Harpers, 1933.

individual who, aside from his interest in the collection of beautiful objects of art, was given over to the end of exercising a sway over men and institutions and of adding to his own fortune.

There could be no picture so completely false as that. The same observation applies to his son, the late Mr. J. P. Morgan, who inherited the great public spirit that his father had and, in his own day and generation—particularly throughout World War I and the reconstruction years that followed it—rendered an immense public service and leadership. At the time his services were better understood than in the case of his father, but they, too, have never been properly chronicled. Mr. J. P. Morgan, the younger, was, to be sure, in his prime somewhat less active than his father had been and than some of his partners were. But the firm could have accomplished little without his steadying judgment and his firm determination to serve the interests of his country.

It was the association of these two men and of the others that they chose to work with them that, for over thirty-five years, made the Morgan banking office for me the most interesting and stimulating spot in the world — not in the routine of borrowing or lending money, which any first-class bank organization can carry out — but in the opportunities for constructive work that have been thrust upon the group centered there.

II

The First World War

6

OUTBREAK OF WORLD WAR I

The outbreak of World War I came barely sixteen months after Mr. J. Pierpont Morgan's death in late March of 1913. Mr. J. P. Morgan, who had quickly taken up the leadership in the community that his father had laid down at his death, was especially familiar with European conditions. He had served several years of banking apprenticeship in London, with his grandfather's firm, J. S. Morgan & Co., and its successor, Morgan Grenfell & Co., Ltd.

It was Mr. J. P. Morgan's hope, up to the very end, that war would be averted. When there came the threatening days of late July, 1914, and it was first proposed that the New York Stock Exchange be closed, Mr. Morgan had advised against such action. At a meeting of bankers and Stock Exchange executives at our offices on Thursday afternoon, July 30, 1914, sentiment was likewise against closing the Exchange. But the developments of the next twenty-four hours determined its necessity, and Mr. Morgan took for him the unusual course of giving out a statement as follows:

Friday, July 31, 1914
Alarming as the news is from Europe, I am still hoping there

will not be a general war. While the gravity of the present situation can hardly be exaggerated, there is still the opportunity for the sober second-thought of the people of Europe to prevail over their first impulses. If the delicate situation can be held in abeyance for a few days, I should expect a rising tide of protest from the people who are to pay for war with their blood and their property.

The situation of the American security markets during the past two days has been a splendid illustration of the inherent soundness of financial conditions in this country. While we all earnestly hoped that the New York Stock Exchange might be kept open, the situation is fraught with so much uncertainty that it seemed necessary in the interests of the whole country to close the Exchange.

It is essentially a time for the owners of American securities to keep their heads. Bear in mind that the actual properties represented by American securities will not suffer greatly by a European war. During the past few days the American people have been buying back American securities at low prices. Presumably they will pay for those securities with their wheat and other products at high prices.

It is idle to say that America will not be hurt by a general European war. The wholesale waste of capital involved in such a catastrophe would result in a distribution of losses the world over, but the loss here would be infinitesimal compared with the losses to the countries immediately involved. There is no doubt that the whole American people will cooperate to restore normal conditions throughout the country at the earliest possible moment.

World War I was not just a mischance. Germany had long been yearning for it. It is clear that the disastrous conflict started on a schedule laid down long before. The Germans planned it that way. Throughout all the confused and threatening days that ensued after the assassination of the Austrian heir apparent, Archduke Franz Ferdinand, on June 28, 1914, Lord Grey, Britain's foreign minister and other Allied diplomats worked desperately to keep the peace. But not for nothing had the Prussian officers at evening mess been for years pledging to one another "Der Tag."

Austria's declaration of war against Serbia on July 28, 1914, was followed by a general scramble for mobilization of troops by most of the leading European countries. Yet even as general war became a certainty, thoughtful men were still asking themselves what in the world there was to fight about. Germany's domestic economy was prospering. Her foreign trade was constantly making new records in volume and profit. She was building up her navy steadily and satisfactorily, and though Britain was uneasy over this development there was absolutely nothing that she could do about it — and she did nothing. Thus to the world at large, amazed and still unbelieving in the sixty days prior to the outbreak, Germany's sudden invasion of helpless Belgium on August 3rd came as an enormous shock.

What about the almost century-old treaty (1839) that pledged Germany with the other powers to preserve Belgium's neutrality? The answer of Germany's Foreign Minister, Bethmann-Hollweg, was simple and Teutonic: What was a treaty anyway but a "scrap of paper"? Britain, under her obligations, had no recourse save to go to Belgium's rescue, and so on August 4, 1914, declared war on Germany. Before the end of the first week in August war had been declared between Germany and Austria on the one side, and Russia, Serbia, Belgium, France and Britain on the other. The die was cast.

Many writers are fond of saying that economic factors

are chiefly responsible for bringing on wars. That statement has never been true. It is not true today. In Germany's case in 1914, her own increasing well-being, instead of being an incentive for her to keep the peace, only seemed to make her all the more eager to seize from her neighbors their lands and property by a war of conquest.

Although almost three years were to elapse before Germany drove America into the war, the outbreak of the world conflict had immediate financial and economic effects on America which it may be of interest to note briefly. The markets of the world generally, commercial and financial, had been knocked into a cocked hat, and international exchange was brought to an abrupt halt. America began to feel the pinch at once. Her merchants had obligations falling due in London. Normally they could have covered themselves by buying sterling at the rate of a pound sterling to $4.8665. But the market was almost bare of sterling bills, and American debtors, in order to avoid default, bid as high as $7 in exchange for the pound.

More serious than these difficulties of private firms or individuals was the plight of the City of New York. It owed in London and in Paris something above $77,000,000 that it had borrowed direct, not through the intermediation of bankers. The City had sold its notes in those markets because of the lower rates of interest prevailing there than at home. But New York City's bills were falling due within a few weeks and the wherewithal to meet them was lacking, for they were payable not in dollars but in sterling and in francs.

There was some loose talk of New York City declaring simply that "the exigencies of the war prevented payment." To Mr. J. P. Morgan, his immediate associates, and to the New York banking world generally, the idea of any such repudiation was unthinkable. So, with the anxious support of the New York municipal authorities, Mr. Morgan got in touch with the Federal Reserve Bank and the Secretary of the Treasury at Washington, to suggest their approval of the organization of a New York banking syndicate that would pledge sufficient gold to meet the City's payments, even if the banks were thereby obliged to dip into their normal gold reserves. The Federal authorities at once said yes. They wisely decided that gold bank reserves were useless unless they could be utilized to meet the very emergencies for which by law they had been established. The Morgan banking firm then invited Messrs. Kuhn, Loeb & Co. to join with it in forming the rescue syndicate. The transaction was promptly completed, although not without some difficulties, and New York City's credit was saved. In this whole operation the late Dwight W. Morrow of our firm was exceedingly active and resourceful.

Not many weeks thereafter purchases of supplies by the Allies in the United States began on a heavy scale, the demand for dollars increasing as that for sterling and francs declined. Thus the exchange between New York and London and Paris soon readjusted itself. After all these years and in the face of immense increase in the volume of financial transactions, both government and private, this crisis of thirty-three years ago sounds of minor importance. But at the time, with the anxiety of the Federal and municipal authorities, plus that of the banking world, to preserve the credit of America's leading city, there was great concern. Corresponding relief came when the crisis was met.

Meanwhile the attitude of the Wilson Administration at Washington was to urge the greatest possible neutrality in respect to the combatants. On August 18, 1914, President Wilson made a statement in which he urged the American people to be strictly "impartial in thought as well as in action." This injunction, having to do with the innermost reflections and sympathies of our citizens, was rather a tall order.

By far the greatest single group of individuals in America was of Anglo-Saxon descent. To many of them, even though they were anxious not to become involved in the war, Germany's outrageous invasion of Belgium, and her apparent determination upon the ruthless conquest of France, put her in a class by herself. Of course as a partial offset there were thousands of German-American citizens who were naturally strong for their old fatherland. American interest in the European war generally was lively east of the Allegheny Mountains. In the Middle West it was lukewarm. In the Far West (not the Pacific Coast) it was of such secondary interest that the local press frequently carried its war news on an inside page.

The conflict had started badly for the Allies, and Germany's swift invasion of Northern France seemed altogether likely to encircle Paris. Yet on the Western front, almost by a miracle, General Joffre of France in

September of 1914 turned back the Germans at the Marne, thus giving a breathing space for French army reorganization and for lively recruiting in Britain which had entered the war wholly unprepared for land fighting, and with such meagre forces available to send to France that Marshal French's little army was known as the "Contemptibles." Yet they and the French fought with dogged vigor and held back the Germans, to the surprise and fury of the German High Command.

Regarding this first battle of the Marne in the autumn of 1914, J. P. Morgan told me of a conversation that he once had with King George V who said to him, "I am not sure that I was able to render any real service to my country in World War I, with the possible exception of one occasion. It was," he said, "just after the enemy forces had gathered for the first battle of the Marne. In the middle of the night I was awakened by a dispatch from Marshal French, commander of the British Expeditionary Force, saying that the French (General Joffre) were begging him to join them in an immediate attack, but that his troops were ill prepared, low in arms and ammunition, and disaster seemed almost inevitable. 'What is your Majesty's view?' French asked." The King said: "I sent a dispatch in reply immediately, saying 'You can do naught else but fight for King and country.'" It was plain enough that Marshal French was waiting for some decisive word. Upon receipt of the King's telling message Marshal French threw his "Contemptibles" into the battle. The Germans were turned back. France was saved.

Even after the early years, the course of the struggle

57

with a few notable exceptions continued to go badly for the Allies. The initial surprise and jump that the Germans had effected, had almost won the war at the start. To turn the scale was a long, slow, discouraging job for the Allies.

7

ALLIED PURCHASING IN AMERICA

As purchases in America by the Allies of grain, cotton, steel, and all sorts of supplies began mounting rapidly, they came to be a very considerable factor in stimulating American agriculture and industry which had been rather in the doldrums. To many American men of affairs it was, however, becoming clear that the Allied purchasing was not being conducted systematically nor economically. Britain's helter-skelter and at times almost frantic buying, lacking method and system, failed to serve her own purposes, and was calculated to upset the markets generally.

The Allies were paying fantastically high commissions to a miscellaneous lot of brokers. The buying was heavy, but so spasmodic that American producers were bewildered. They were anxious that the Allies should carry on their business in a more orderly manner, even under the dreadful emergency of war. The desired end seemed impossible to attain. The Allies, with the traditional ineptitude that allies display, were competing briskly against one another, the British against the French, both countries against the Russians; the British Army vying with the Admiralty in the same markets.

Finally, the supply situation, vitally important as it was for the Allies, became so confused that, at the urging of Mr. Morgan and his other partners of J. P. Morgan & Co., Mr. Henry P. Davison in late 1914 went to London and suggested to the British authorities that they bring order out of chaos and concentrate their American buying. Mr. Lloyd George, who was the most active member of the British Cabinet, was strongly for the new plan. The upshot was that the British entrusted their miscellaneous buying to our firm, with notable exceptions in the line of wheat, of horses, etc. The Allies had been paying buying commissions on a varying scale, ranging up to 7½%. We proposed a commission of 2% from which we were to pay all our expenses.

We persuaded the late Edward R. Stettinius (then president of the Diamond Match Company) to take charge of the work. He did a most outstanding job, so arduous that shortly after the end of the war he broke down and died, although not an old man. So far as possible Stettinius persuaded all the Allies to pool their requirements. He instituted competitive bidding from American producers and was thus able to reduce selling prices to reasonable figures. This gave all concerned the advantage of strictly business transactions in place of harum-scarum scrambling for goods, with the Allies running up the markets on themselves.

Throughout the earlier months of the Purchasing Contract, matters went steadily, but not very satisfactorily, at the London end of the line. In the midst of decisions pressing on the high command, replies to our messages were at times unduly delayed, with consequent loss in cost and availability of goods to Britain. Lord Kitchener, the hero of Khartoum a generation before, was Minister of War. He was a better fighter than he was administrator. He had thought at the start that Britain's total purchases in America would not amount to more than $50,000,000. In May of 1915, however, the magnetic Lloyd George became Minister of Munitions. Within twenty-four hours we could detect a definite change, a speeding up of operations in the field of supply all along the line.

At one time in London, after the arrangement had been under way for some months, Mr. Lloyd George said to Mr. Davison: "Look here, my good man, you must be sure, you know, to try to even up orders between Democrat and Republican producers." "My dear Mr. Minister," replied Mr. Davison, "there is no politics in our office or in this business of purchasing for the Allies. We don't know Republicans from Democrats. We would place orders with a Socialist if he happened to have the best supplies at the lowest prices to our clients." The Minister had no more to say.

In July, 1915, a desperate attempt was made on Mr. Morgan's life. Some miscreant made his way into the entrance of the Morgan home on the north shore of Long Island just as Mr. Morgan and his wife were walking down the hall. Mrs. Morgan was the first to see the pistol in the man's hand. She threw herself in front of her husband who then too caught sight of the weapon, shoved his wife aside, rushed upon the intruder and bore him to the floor. Although two bullets from the assassin's revolver struck Mr. Morgan, the wounds were in no wise serious, and within a few weeks he was again at his office. His own presence of mind and overpowering rush upon his assailant had saved his life. Arrested, the would-be assassin was confined in one of the local jails where he managed to commit suicide. Whether he was attempting to avoid disclosure of his principals; or whether he was working his hand alone, the police never found out. The general assumption was that the attempt on Mr. Morgan's life was a feeble effort to cripple in some way the purchasing plans of the Allies.

In due course the British Government very properly sent out one of their top men of affairs, D. A. Thomas (afterwards Lord Rhondda), to make an inspection of the Purchasing Agency workings, to look into complaints, which were difficult to answer in Parliament, to the effect that the British Government's representatives were not accessible to various people having supplies to offer. Davison assured Mr. Thomas that the more he went to the mat, the greater service he would render to his principals and also to J. P. Morgan & Co.

Mr. Thomas installed himself and a staff of secretaries at the Plaza Hotel on 59th Street, but spent much of his time at our offices taking part in the highly important discussions with representatives of the various companies. All the books, contracts, all correspondence, and all documents and memoranda having to do with the purchases for the British Government account were turned over to Mr. Thomas, and he was encouraged to join Mr. Stettinius in his negotiations with various possible contractors and producers. At the end of a few weeks, Mr. Thomas came downtown and with considerable heat announced that he was "through investigating." He said that he had enough of such work, and he declared that the services of our firm were of such a character as to make any real criticism of its activities baseless. He had had long lines of people forming at his door, each professing to have some cause of complaint or grievance. After careful investigation, he had nowhere found the slightest basis for complaint.

For a few moments in that three weeks of Mr. Thomas's visit, he had, I recall, a distinctly uncomfortable time. We had furnished him, as I have said, with copies of correspondence bearing upon British purchases. The arrangement was hardly well started before one morning his secretary in great distress called on the telephone from the Plaza Hotel, saying that a sudden gust of wind had blown one particularly important memorandum out of the window. A subordinate British official reached the window in time to see the flying paper disappear amid the traffic of Fifth Avenue. To the British officials it seemed vital that the memorandum, written on three sheets of onion-skin paper pinned together, should not get into German hands. So concerned was Mr. Thomas that he cabled to Mr. Lloyd George, reporting the loss.

One of the Morgan firm's staff promptly gathered a group of searchers, and for hours they combed the whole neighborhood. In the late afternoon came a heavy rain, and that was the end of the three sheets of onion-skin paper. They were, of course, never found. To reassure Mr. Thomas, members of his staff took three sheets of onion-skin paper similarly put together, and trailed them through the water in his bath tub. Their speedy disintegration made Mr. Thomas feel better. The whole incident sounded as if it might have been taken from an Oppenheim novel.

When America was forced to declare war in April, 1917, the firm of J. P. Morgan & Co. turned over promptly to our Government the entire purchasing operation. Mr. Stettinius was asked to become an Assistant Secretary of War, and in that position in Washington, and later abroad, he did work of great value in coordinating further the demands and the purchases of the Allied Governments. Little has ever been said of the greatest work of all that Stettinius accomplished for his country. That was through the education of many American manufacturers to the task of supplying certain forms of munitions, so that when Germany finally drove us into the conflict our country had had at least a certain amount of preparation in the field of war production.

8

END OF AMERICAN NEUTRALITY

The *Lusitania* was torpedoed and sunk, with the loss of many American citizens, in May, 1915. President Wilson transmitted messages of protest to Germany, but took no stronger action. However, the months following the sinking of the *Lusitania* revealed a growing tenseness of feeling in America regarding the war. Most Americans, on whichever side their sympathies lay, had long before dismissed the possibility of neutrality "in thought" that the President had advocated. To a great section of American public opinion, President Wilson's well-rounded verbal protests to Germany sounded inadequate.

Many groups now began to agitate the question of how, with the approval of the Federal Government, some aid could be provided for the Allies without involvement in war itself. It was, in fact, the same question that came up in the early years of World War II when the Administration at Washington began to concern itself actively as to what it could do "short of war" to aid the Allies against Germany. Back in 1915 this question was not being asked by our Administration, but by individuals and groups of citizens who were moved primarily by sympathy for the Allied cause. This feeling was perhaps emphasized when the agricultural and business communities began to realize that Britain, in meeting her rapidly mounting payments here, was exhausting her supply of quick assets consisting of gold and of American securities that she had commandeered from her own citizens and was carefully liquidating on the American markets.

Mr. James J. Hill, that great old pioneer who almost single-handed built the Great Northern Railway from St. Paul to the Coast, was strongly in favor of a sizable loan to Britain. The hard-headed way that he put it to Mr. Morgan and his partners was that if the Allies had to stop purchases here for lack of credit, the American farmers "were likely to secure for their wheat only fifty cents a bushel against the price of a dollar that they might otherwise receive." Then Mr. Hill added: "If our farmers were prepared to sell seven or eight hundred thousand bushels of wheat the country could afford to lose the entire amount of a loan rather than have the Allies forced out of the market here for foodstuffs." This was rather oversimplifying the proposition, but Mr. Hill's influence through the West and Northwest was great. He would be a help in any sound loan proposition that the investment houses might devise.

Mr. J. P. Morgan, however, was considering the whole situation in other terms. Years later, in 1936, when he and his partners were haled before a Committee of the United States Senate to explain in detail what the Morgan firm had done to further the cause of the Allies in World War I, he made at the very start a statement that explained simply and clearly his point of view, that of his partners, and that of millions of other Americans. Mr. Morgan said:

> When in 1914 the war was begun by Germany . . . we were deeply shocked. None of us had expected such a course to be taken by any civilized nation, and in spite of President Wilson's urging impartiality "even in thought" we found it quite impossible to be impartial as between right and wrong. . . . We agreed that we should do all that was lawfully in our power to help the Allies win the war as soon as possible. That thought was the fundamental idea underlying everything that we did from the beginning of the struggle till the Armistice in November, 1918.

As the need of the Allies for credit facilities here to help meet their growing purchases increased, the Morgan firm suggested to the British authorities that they explore the possibilities for obtaining a loan. Early in September, 1915, an Anglo-French mission, headed by Lord Reading (formerly Sir Rufus Isaacs), Lord Chief Justice of England, arrived in New York, and sent word that they would like to confer with us. Mr. J. P. Morgan, Mr. Henry P. Davison and I promptly entered into discussions that continued for over three weeks. The final result was the notable Anglo-French loan, the public issue of $500,000,000 of 5% Five-Year bonds, being the joint and several obligations of the British and French Governments. A country-wide syndicate of investment houses and banks under the leadership of the Morgan firm underwrote the issue, which was an immediate success. Our firm took a share in the underwriting, but declined to accept any compensation for handling and managing the business.

Lord Reading proved himself an able negotiator, although he had rather a difficult team to handle in the make-up of the mixed Commission, and he was sometimes bothered more by small questions than by large ones. He showed great tact in his handling of the whole matter of the Anglo-American loan in an atmosphere that in some parts of the country was by no means cordial to it. When the loan had been underwritten and success was assured, Lord Reading decided that it would be wise for him and one or two of his colleagues to visit Chicago and meet some of the leaders of the community there — especially as sixty per cent of the proceeds of the proposed loan would be spent in the Mississippi Valley. I was deputed to escort Lord Reading and his party out to Chicago.

The visit was intended to gain good-will, but not material investment support for the loan. All the Chicago banks, except one, had already declined to have any share in the underwriting of the loan, on the ground that thousands of Germanophile depositors had threatened, in case of the bank's participation, to withdraw their accounts. The one exception to which I have just alluded was the bank headed by Charles G. Dawes, later General Pershing's aide in France during the war and from 1924 to 1928 Vice President of the United States and later Ambassador to the Court of St. James's. He declared that the loan would benefit America and that he wanted to share in it. His bank lost a few depositors, but they were far more than offset by new ones who approved Dawes' attitude.

The Chicago leaders had arranged a banquet for Lord

Reading, not, they were careful to explain, as head of the Anglo-French Loan Mission, but as Lord Chief Justice of England. Indeed, that Chicago audience started out by way of being exceedingly cold to Lord Reading. When he was introduced to speak, he was greeted with a respectful, but not a warmhearted, clapping of hands.

Lord Reading did not attempt to talk much about the loan. He spoke of it, to be sure. He pointed it out as a necessity, if the purchases of his Government from our farmers and merchants were to continue on a large scale. But he did not ask for Chicago's cooperation. What he did say was more effective. He declared that it was a rare privilege for him to be in Chicago, and he went on to describe how, years before, he had come near making his home in Chicago. It seems that as a growing lad, just finished with his schooling, he had determined to come to America and to make his way in the New World. He had decided to settle in Chicago. His trunk was packed and he was about to sail from Liverpool, when, suddenly, the death of a near relative changed all his plans and kept him in England.

And, as Lord Reading told the story, he almost seemed to say: "Ah, my friends, who knows but that, if instead of stopping in lowly England, pursuing the dull round of the law and finally attaining a mere Lord Chief Justiceship, I might have come out here, have settled in your midst, — who knows, I say, but that I should have been a happier and at least a better man today!"

The loans by American investors to the Allied Governments aroused great interest in financial circles and excitement in Washington. To us in these days when billions of dollars are being tossed about with seeming nonchalance by the Federal Government, the figures seem almost trifling. But over thirty years ago things were different. While, too, the issues of the war were gradually becoming clearer, especially to people on the Atlantic seaboard, Washington's attitude was rather sullenly acquiescent towards these operations, although there was no law to prevent them. Needless to say, the American bankers committed themselves to no Allied loan operations without first receiving the approval — no matter how grudging — of the Administration at Washington.

For the members of our firm, believing thoroughly in the Allied cause and determined to do all we could, with Washington's approval, to further that cause, these months from the autumn of 1915 (Anglo-French loan) to our entry into the war in April, 1917, were crowded day and night with incessant labor involved in the negotiation of the Allied loans themselves and the formation of banking syndicates to underwrite the issues. The operations, however, were so sound in themselves, and the Germans were so steadily ruining their own cause with the American public, that our task became steadily less difficult as the months wore on to the climax of President Wilson's request for a declaration of war in early April, 1917.

The President's dream of holding America free from German aggression, by speaking softly to Berlin and frowning upon Allied financing here, was rudely shattered when, on January 31, 1917, along came a German note announcing unrestricted submarine warfare. This was the sort of handwriting on the wall that no one could ignore. From this time on, German-American relations steadily worsened. Changing with the shift of the wind, the Federal Reserve Board on March 8, 1917, executed an about-face on the subject of Allied financing against which they had warned the American banking community the previous November. The Board now expressed its desire "to make clear that it did not seek to create an unfavorable attitude on the part of American investors toward desirable foreign securities, and to emphasize the point that American funds available for investment may, with advantage to the country's foreign trade and the domestic economic situation, be employed in the purchase of such securities."

Germany's declaration of unrestricted submarine warfare brought to an end the President's endeavor to hold the balance even between Germany and the Allies, and to keep America out of the conflict. On April 4, 1917, President Wilson addressed a joint session of Congress, declaring that Germany was making war upon us, and calling for the recognition of such a state of conflict. Two days later, April 6th, with only a few dissenting votes, Congress ratified the American Declaration of War upon the common foe of Western civilization.

For me in my early forties those years of World War I, before and after America became a participant, were bound to be crowded and thrilling. The heavy burdens thrust upon us, or that we chose to assume, were, however, largely offset by the apparent advantage to our own country as well as to the Allied cause from the loan operations.

My most active partner, Henry P. Davison, was drafted in early 1917 as the head of the American Red Cross. He moved to Washington and became the moving spirit in all the immense development of Red Cross activities; the spearhead of all its great and successful drives for funds. He helped America, always generous-minded, to set a new and far higher standard of giving for public causes than ever before. He it was who when the Red Cross directors first approached him to head the organization and said, "Our first drive for funds if well handled ought to yield $10,000,000," exclaimed: "Ten million dollars! One hundred million, you mean." And $100,000,000 it was, $114,000,000 in fact.

With Davison at Washington, and Edward Stettinius, the elder, in charge of purchases for the Allies, there fell upon the rest of us most of the negotiation and work in the Allied loan operations. Then the moment that America entered the conflict we became engrossed deeply with our Government in its own war financing. Mr. Morgan and I served upon the Liberty Loan Committees, and I was drafted to do a considerable amount of public speaking. It was a novel experience for America to be engaged in a great war, particularly on foreign soil. Some of our elders there were that still recalled the days of our own great Civil War. But the middle-aged and those of draft years had largely to blaze their own way. The art of propaganda at that time happily fell far short of its present-day excesses, and its operations bore a rather amateur flavor.

Before we entered the war the British Government had been wise enough to obtain invitations for some of their men of letters to visit and lecture in this country. These men, for example, John Masefield, now the British Poet Laureate, made no direct attempt to induce this country to enter the conflict. What they did chiefly was to read to eager public audiences from their own works; to render a vivid portrayal of Britain in wartime; or now and then — as in the case of Mr. Masefield, who had been a stretcher-bearer in the early days of the war — to give a glimpse of the exposed and battered front line in France. It was Masefield's poem, "August 1914," that painted so touching a picture of the English countryside and of its countrymen as they were moved by war from their ancient and simple pastimes to the wretchedness and desolation of sudden death overseas:

> *And died (uncouthly, most) in foreign lands*
> *For some idea but dimly understood*
> *Of an English city never built by hands*
> *Which love of England prompted and made good.*

In that World War I there were almost half a score of those young British poets that came suddenly into brilliant flowering — men like Siegfried Sassoon, Robert Nichols and Rupert Brooke, who died on a Grecian isle in the service of the Royal Navy. We all remember Rupert Brooke's perhaps most oft quoted lines:

> *If I should die, think only this of me:*
> *That there's some corner of a foreign field*
> *That is for ever England.*

It was not hard to understand that what they wrote and read aloud to us Americans kindled afresh our glowing memories of England as she had been in the past, and moved us to even greater zeal to prepare our country to do its share in stamping out the Teutonic evil.

I recently asked a British man of letters why it was that World War II had never produced a crop of stirring young poets as in World War I, to arouse imagination and to quicken our hearts. "The reason is clear," he said. "World War I we looked upon in Britain as a glorious crusade. We were saving Belgium and helping to rescue France from an evil thing that had set out to destroy both countries — to which so much of British civilization itself was indebted. World War II, on the contrary, was not a crusade. It was nothing to grow lyric about. It was just a job, an extraordinarily difficult, dangerous and nasty job that just had to be done."

9

TRIP TO EUROPE IN 1917

In the autumn of 1917 President Wilson asked Colonel E. M. House to head a small mission to visit England and France and to consult with the authorities there on matters economic, financial, and even military. By then America had had six months of armed conflict, but our land forces had not as yet seen action. On sea our Navy and particularly our destroyers had done a first-class job against the German submarines. Time had not sufficed, however, to train and equip our men for the overseas fighting, and while we had some small arms we were without the necessary artillery and ammunition.

Lacking trained financial men on a staff level in Washington, the Administration sent me word they would be glad if I would volunteer to be in London and Paris at the same time as the House Mission, and thus be available as confidential unofficial adviser on any phase of that mission's task. Washington felt that my acquaintance with many of the active personalities in the Allied Governments might be of some advantage. The President, however, preferred that no public mention of my connection with the Mission should be made. I will confess that for a few minutes such an attitude gave me pause. However, Mr. Morgan promptly endorsed my own decision, which was that if I could serve the cause in any way I must do so.

The trip across the Atlantic, following the House Mission by a few days, turned out to be delightful because of our fellow passengers. We had a rough crossing on the little old *New York* of the American line. It was with considerable relief that, twenty-four hours from land, we came on deck one bright sunny morning to find four jaunty destroyers, flying the American flag, tossing and rolling in the waves around us, and prepared to escort us safely through the submarine zone to Liverpool, where we arrived next day.

I had with me George Whitney of our office staff, now president of the Morgan bank, and who then had a far more detailed knowledge of many financial questions than I. Lord Reading, who had become British Ambassador at Washington, and his wife were aboard, as was also Lord Northcliffe, then proprietor and publisher of the London *Times*. It was here, too, that I first met Thomas Catto, acting for the British Government on important commercial matters. Later Catto was an immense success as manager for several years of Andrew Yule & Co. in India; after that one of our partners in Morgan Grenfell & Co. of London; drafted from there to the British Treasury for most of World War II; and finally made Governor of the Bank of England.

I must interject here an anecdote that has to do with Lord Catto. During the recent war, shortly after the heroic and successful defense of Stalingrad, he received

a phone call from an old colleague who had been associated with him in the years before World War I in
representing a British firm at Batum in the Caucasus.
"And what do you think of Zhukoff now?" the caller
asked.

"Whom do you mean — that very active Russian
Marshal that won glory at Stalingrad? Why do you
mention him?"

"Don't you remember little Zhukoff," retorted his
old colleague, "that lazy, good-for-nothing office boy
that we had in Batum back in 1912?"

"Don't tell me," exclaimed Lord Catto, "that Marshal
Zhukoff, the star of the Russian army, is that idle young
fellow we could never persuade to do a stroke of work!"

"No mistake," was the reply, "that was the boy that
has become the father of the man — the great Russian
military leader, full of energy, skill and prowess."

It was Marshal Smuts of South Africa who related
this little anecdote to me. "That only goes to show,"
he added, "that you must not conclude that a young lad,
no good at office routine, may not have the making of
a great leader in some other field."

London in November of 1917 was chill and overcast.
Yet it had plenty of life and there was no wringing of
hands over the dangerous developments in Russia, France
and Italy. There was hanging over London, however,
a pall not of this earth, but rather of the shades of hundreds of thousands of the young and gallant Englishmen
that had thrown themselves into the struggle to preserve
freedom, and had fallen on the blood-and-rain-soaked
fields of Flanders.

The House Mission was taking things rather easily, but on the whole covering a good deal of ground with the British authorities. I found myself welcomed from both quarters. There was work to do, but plenty of time for other things, such as the day I spent at golf with Lord Northcliffe, who said he had arranged for me to make a visit to the British front, whenever I crossed to France.

During this stay in London in December, 1917, there were two individuals whom I came to know for the first time and whose friendship has meant much to me during many years of my life. The first was John Buchan (destined twenty years later to be Lord Tweedsmuir and Governor General of Canada). Buchan was perhaps the most versatile man that I had ever met. He had a great talent for sympathy and friendship. A lowland Scot, son of the manse, he had at his tongue's end all the matchless folklore of the Scottish border. He had been in France and Flanders as London *Times* correspondent in the World War, then back to London to head the British Ministry of Information where I had my first contacts with him. John Buchan's friendship, begun in those dark days of World War I and unchanging through the years, was one of the bright spots of my active life.

The other fast friendship gained in the London gloom at that time was with Montagu Norman (now Lord Norman), then deputy governor of the Bank of England over whose activities as governor he was soon to preside for a quarter century or more. Norman had fought in the Boer War and had had several years of

American banking with the old and honorable firm of Brown Brothers & Co. in New York. His later brilliant progress in the City of London led him to activity in the Bank of England. One of my London partners, Edward Grenfell (later Lord St. Just), a director of the Bank, often got Norman and me together at his bachelor home for dinner. Afterward we three huddled around a small grate fire in the library, the only fire in the house, and there and then Norman expounded to me the financial and fiscal situations of the governments involved in the War. As I heard him talk he sounded to me like one of the wisest men in the world, and indeed I have always given him that rating. Governor Norman was of course a conspicuous and indispensable figure in the post-war reconstruction of Europe. In the twenties I saw much of him in connection with the Dawes and Young bond plans designated to assist Germany in her reparation difficulties.

It was early in December of 1917 that the House Mission moved on to Paris. Such discussions as I was asked to take part in were for the most part at the Ministry of Finance and at the Banque de France. M. Ribot, an exceedingly kindly old gentleman, was Minister of Finance at the time. He was grateful for the assistance that American investors and bankers had been able to render to his country prior to America's entry into the war, and his current relations with the American Treasury were running smoothly and well.

I was much moved by my talk with Georges Clemenceau, newly made Premier. His seventy-six years had failed to weaken him, and the "Tiger," as he was called,

79

made a deep impression. With his indomitable and desperate "will to victory," he had been summoned to rescue his country from its disaffection and reverses, slackness, and even partial pacifism. The Bolshevik Revolution and Russia's withdrawal from the war had also come as a great shock to the French people.

Clemenceau plunged into the turbulent stream that was threatening to sweep away the props of the state. He planted himself four square against the heavy current, and stood there like a great, massive rock that could not be moved, a mighty fortress that could not be shaken. He brushed aside the petty troubles and met the great ones head on. No individual in modern history proved to be more the man of the hour than Clemenceau in those critical days of late 1917. For a spur to his own dogged resolution he had all the bitter memories of Germany's conquest of France in the days of his youth.

In the early dusk of that gloomy December day in 1917, M. Clemenceau came forward to greet me with outstretched hands. He was grateful for our expression of the ancient friendship between France and America, shown in the early years of the war; he rejoiced that my countrymen would soon be fighting by the side of his own. He spoke in moving terms of the help that the American Red Cross was already rendering direct to his beloved soldiers. Old, grim and undaunted, Clemenceau at that moment was France in its most gallant mood.

The trip to the British front, arranged by Lord Northcliffe for George Whitney and me, took up several hurried and long-drawn-out days. We motored from

Paris to our headquarters at a château to the eastward. We were of course not to visit the front line trenches, but rather to get such a survey of the whole line as to give us an idea of the strategy that the Allies were pursuing. Early each morning we would set out in an open motor-car, scheduled to visit a series of areas along the British front. Everywhere the going was bad. As we moved towards the much fought over Vimy Ridge, bumping through the broken roads, we more than once found ourselves in a sector where we could hear both German and Allied artillery.

The desolation of the Flanders plain, broken by the water-filled bomb craters, where so many thousands of the Allied troops had laid down their lives, was complete. Had it not been for the boom of artillery, our journey would have seemed to traverse a vast Dantesque Inferno, with frequent flashes from the guns like the fires of the underworld. Nowhere was there a vestige of the glory of war: only the grim and broken land to bring home to us the miseries and sufferings that the Allied troops had endured for months and even years on end. Our daily journeyings across those desolate areas of the Front Line served to show the utter misery, the squalor, the wretchedness that the fighting men had to endure.

While I was still on the Continent, General Charles G. Dawes, at this time General Pershing's aide in charge of the procurement of supplies in Europe, asked me to motor down to Chaumont to visit the General and himself. General Pershing, General Dawes and I had a pleasant talk at Chaumont, at the end of which Dawes said to me, "Tom, I want you to stay over here and become the active scouting officer for the procurement division. You know all the people over here. You are a business man. You can save millions of dollars for the Government. We need you."

I replied that nothing would give me the satisfaction that such a job would; that I should accept it without a moment's hesitation if I did not think that I could do the cause more good by my work in the United States; and if, furthermore, I had not in mind an American who had been a most intimate friend since my boyhood days at Phillips Exeter Academy and Harvard, and who could do a better job than I because he had had legal training.

That was Jeremiah Smith, Jr., of Boston, whose grandfather had been a friend of Washington's, had been Governor of New Hampshire, Chief Justice of that State, and a leading citizen of the country. By his second marriage very late in life, he begat Jeremiah Smith, Jerry's father, in 1837. This son of Jeremiah the First was the most entertaining man I think that I ever met.

Jerry, as everybody called him, was having a highly successful career at the bar in Boston. He was a rugged New Englander, of extraordinary rectitude and some considerable pride in his admirable ancestry. He was intensely patriotic, had at the age of forty-seven spent weeks of training at Plattsburg, and as to the war was quite ready to be commissioned to duty on any front.

"Jerry Smith," I said, "is a man of extraordinary ability and character, knows the languages, a man whose very simplicity carries him through all barriers. He is longing to come over here to render service. He would be better for your job, General Pershing, than any other American I know. Certainly better than myself." General Pershing reached for a cable blank, asked me for Jerry's address, and transmitted then and there a captain's commission for him to equip himself, report to Washington, and come out as soon as possible.

All this Jerry did, and I saw him only a few days before he sailed from New York in December of 1917. I am writing all this to indicate Jerry Smith's gradual emergence into public affairs. He did a splendid job for General Pershing and General Dawes, ranged all over Europe for his supplies, and was just winding up his work when I arrived at Paris in 1919 for the Peace Conference. I at once asked that he be attached as one of the counsellors to the American Commission to Negotiate Peace. This was done, and Jerry proved a sound and excellent aide throughout all the complex negotiations. When the Treaty was completed, he refused to go out to Versailles to see the signing. "It is a poor treaty," said Jerry dourly, "and I don't want to see it signed, thank you."

Less than a year later when the Government asked me to go to Japan and China to handle matters for the International Consortium on China, I begged Jerry to go along as my aide, which he did as I indicate in a future chapter of this book. He also went with me the next year as my counsellor on a trip to the Mexican capital in 1921 when I had been deputed to negotiate a settlement of the Mexican Government's external debt.

With all this experience, when it became time to appoint a Reparations Commission for Hungary, Jerry

Smith's name was so well known that he was a not unnatural selection. He went over to Budapest in 1924.
Sir Arthur Salter in his recent book on *Personality in
Politics* has written briefly on Jerry's term of office at
Budapest, showing his simplicity and his disregard for
formality. In Budapest Jerry Smith created a considerable sensation by refusing to occupy the palace that the
Hungarian Government had set aside for him, saying
that he did not want the Government to waste its money
on a staff of servants for him. He preferred an apart-
ment or a small house where he lived in New England
simplicity and did his job perfectly. The sum total of his
accomplishment is indicated in the fact that he added,
at least for a time, a word to the Hungarian tongue, perhaps also an idea. When a bright new scheme was proposed, purportedly bereft of the usual flim-flam of bargaining, the doubtful would ask, "Come now, is this
absolutely *Jerry?*"

In the autumn of 1927 Jerry accompanied me on a
second trip to the Far East. At the invitation of Japanese
bankers I went out to inspect the recovery that they had
been able to stage after the frightful earthquake and fire
of four years previous. Jerry Smith and I were associated for years on the Board of Trustees of The Phillips
Exeter Academy. He was the one that chose as Principal
of the Academy that outstanding American, Lewis
Perry, and when Jerry died I succeeded him as President
of the Board.

10

THE RUSSIAN REVOLUTION

Just as the House Mission was completing its discussions in Paris in December of 1917, I received an arresting cable message from my old school and business friend, William Boyce Thompson, who was then at Petrograd in charge of the American Red Cross Mission there. He wanted me to meet him in London in order that he might explain the critical Russian situation as he saw it, and the manner in which he believed it might possibly be somewhat ameliorated. I cabled him I would meet him in London as soon as he could get there.

We arrived about the same time, Thompson somewhat breathless and tempest-tossed after a trip from Bergen in a British warship, *Vulture*. Its course lay through a portion of the North Sea in which German submarines had been very active. As Thompson went aboard he was warned that submarines were thick in the offing. But his journey had been tiring and the wait at Bergen tedious. "Let them sink her and be damned," he remarked, "I'm going to sleep." And he slept around the clock.

Thompson's story, when he reached London, was

simple and worth while listening to. Like Senator Root, Thompson had laid his bets on Kerensky, the Socialist Premier. Thompson had spent a million dollars of his own money to further Kerensky's efforts to keep his country in the war. When, however, the extreme Leftists under Lenin and Trotsky had snatched the Government from Kerensky and were busily engaged in trying to administer it and meanwhile were pulling Russia out of the war, Thompson promptly decided to make the best of a bad job, and, through the energetic Raymond Robins of the American Red Cross, established contact with these Bolshevik leaders.

These latter took the attitude, according to Robins,* that Russia had shot her bolt in the war and was finished, but that unless the Germans laid down peace terms that were fair and not too disruptive of the Russian Empire they would, with American help, have another try at fighting. Whether they meant a word of what they said, no one will ever know. Raymond Robins believed they did and Thompson, through the Red Cross at Washington, had continued by cable to bombard the Administration with the same pleas that Senator Root had voiced in the previous summer, namely, to give some tangible evidence in the way of food and relief of that American friendship which President Wilson had, at various stages of the Russian anti-Czarist Revolution since its start eight months before, proclaimed.

Washington being rather lethargic to such cabled pleas, Thompson sought with my aid to find out what the British attitude might be. So I took him the rounds

* See William Hard's book *Raymond Robins' Own Story*, Harpers, 1920, on Robins' experiences with Lenin and Trotsky.

of high officialdom in London. From the start his homely, American straightforward talk made appeal to all of them, — to men like John Buchan (later Lord Tweedsmuir), Sir Edward Carson, close in the confidence of the War Cabinet, Admiral Reginald Hall, that extraordinary individual who was chief of British Naval Intelligence, Lord Reading, Montagu Norman, Governor of the Bank of England, all of them hard-headed men, Sir George Clarke of the Foreign Office (representing Mr. Balfour whose views were later explained by the Prime Minister) and finally to the Prime Minister himself.

We wound up by my taking Thompson for a long breakfast with Mr. Lloyd George at No. 10 Downing Street. The Prime Minister was the most enthusiastic of all. He felt that Sir George Buchanan, the British Ambassador at Petrograd, had been badly misled. Buchanan's irretrievable error had been to support the deposition of Prime Minister Kerensky, quite failing to see that the succeeding Government would inevitably move further to the left instead of to the right. This blunder Mr. Lloyd George felt had been a fatal one.

To Thompson and me the Prime Minister expressed himself as strongly in favor of attempting more active contact and cooperation with the new Soviet Government. He was for no face-saving policy on the part of either Britain or America. He was for something realistic that — even though the chances were against it — might conceivably serve to hold Russia in the war. We were talking through a late December morning that was a gloomy one. The news from the front was not encouraging. Outside the clouds hung from a leaden sky. The Horse Guards Parade just beyond the windows was almost deserted. But Mr. Lloyd George, as he walked up and down the breakfast room at No. 10 Downing Street, rubbing his hands and waxing eloquent, made things almost cheerful as he gave concrete expression to his ideas.

These were, as Mr. Lloyd George put it, that a joint Anglo-American Mission — it might consist of only two or three men — should be sent to Petrograd, should show to the Bolshevik rulers that at least Britain and America still had an interest in Russia, still felt that aid to Russia in keeping her in the war, even though in a purely defensive relation, was well worth while if it would add a featherweight to the possible defeat of the German menace that was threatening all the Allies, including Russia.

Mr. Lloyd George said it was no wonder that the soldiers of the Russian Army, with no weapons, food or warm clothing, badly led almost to the point of treachery — no wonder that they were breaking away and wearily plodding back over the desolate steppes to the homeland. The British people and the Americans must have some understanding of the situation. It was vital to handle it promptly. "You will return, both of you, at once," he said to Colonel Thompson and me, "and see your President. He is full of liberal ideas. He will be ready to act with me."

We must remember that the British Prime Minister was discussing the situation in Russia, not as it has developed in the almost thirty years since the close of World

War I, but as it was when the outcome of World War I was still almost a toss-up. Mr. Lloyd George too recalled with gratitude to Russia her part in the early days of the conflict. When World War I started, the Prime Minister pointed out, it had not been Russia's plan to make an immediate attack on East Prussia. But when in the late summer of 1914 Paris began to be threatened by the German advance in France, the Russian High Command gave orders for the East Prussian invasion. That was the point in Russia's favor that Mr. Lloyd George never forgot.

We of 1947, in recalling the British Prime Minister's eager attitude in 1917, must put ourselves in his shoes and look out of his eyes. When he was speaking the Red Terror had not shown its head, and while the Czar and his family had been sequestrated, their persons were still safe and they were carefully looked after. Some of the most heartrending developments in the Russian scene had not yet taken place. Russia was out of the war largely because her munitions production had fallen away to nothing, the soldiers had no rifles or shoes and the whole army had been swiftly infiltrated by German agents.

Mr. Lloyd George went on to say, "We must do the utmost to arouse the war-weary Russians to the German menace, to the impossible terms of peace that Germany is undoubtedly urging. If no help comes from Allied quarters, the Soviet leaders may be forced to accept those terms. Be sure to see the President promptly," said the Prime Minister. "This is a situation that Mr. Wilson cannot neglect."

So Thompson and I came post-haste home on the liner *Olympic*, zigzagging all across the North Atlantic to avoid the submarines. Once landed on Christmas morning of 1917, Thompson and I started to try to see President Wilson, never doubting that he would readily grant us a brief interview to hear the information that Colonel Thompson had brought through from Petrograd, and to listen to Mr. Lloyd George's message.

But it was not to be. Mr. Wilson refused to see us. He was reported to us as saying he did not want to talk with anyone who would throw away a million dollars, alluding to Colonel Thompson's generous and heroic attempt, as his Red Cross associates thought it was, to try to keep Kerensky in power and Russia in the war as our ally. We went the rounds of Washington and at every point met sympathetic ears. Justice Brandeis of the Supreme Court, whose judgment we understood went far with the President, was exceedingly keen for a trial of Mr. Lloyd George's plan. Frank L. Polk, the Under Secretary of State, was equally clear. So were Secretary of the Treasury McAdoo and George Creel, in charge of Government publicity. They all urged that a small joint commission be formed to establish contact, and at the very least to find out what the situation was for the future guidance of the two governments. This, it was felt, could do no harm: it might be productive of good.

But no: President Wilson felt that he had made his gesture toward Russia in the various public communications that he had uttered, urging upon the Russian people the joys of democratic action. He was, it is only

fair to say, undoubtedly perplexed by the varying reports from different sources. Our Ambassador, David
R. Francis, for example, believed in the Russian people,
he said, but of course was much opposed to the new
Government and thought any effort to try to keep
Russia in the war was futile. Meanwhile, moreover, at
George Creel's suggestion, President Wilson had sent
to Russia Edgar Sisson, editor of *Cosmopolitan* maga-
zine, who after an exceedingly difficult four weeks'
journey reached Petrograd. His assignment was to get
a fresh angle on the situation from the eyes of a trained
journalist.

Thompson and I could hardly believe that Mr. Wilson
would listen neither to Thompson, coming almost direct
from Petrograd, nor to the urgent views of the British
Prime Minister. Finally, however, it was plain that the
effort was hopeless. For the record, Thompson and I
finally transmitted a memorandum to the President sum-
marizing the whole situation. We began by quoting
briefly from his message to Congress December 4, 1917.
In this message the President showed the same unyield-
ing and even naive idealism that characterized so many
of his utterances, namely, his convinced belief that,
given the chance, all men would at once enter the struggle to set up thoroughly democratic processes of government. As applied to the 170 million Russian people,
of course there was no such word as *democracy* in their
language, let alone knowledge among the great mass of
what such a word meant. (The passage of thirty years
has not changed Russia in that respect.) Mr. Wilson,
too, seemed entirely ignorant of the chaos that had

reigned throughout Russia since the early Milyukoff revolution in April, 1917. In his message of December 4, 1917, the President had said:

> But the Congress that concludes this war will feel the full strength of the tides that run now in the hearts and consciences of free men everywhere. Its conclusions will run with those tides.
>
> All these things have been true from the very beginning of this stupendous war: and I cannot help thinking that if they had been made plain at the very outset, the sympathy and enthusiasm of the Russian people might have been once and for all enlisted on the side of the Allies, suspicion and distrust swept away, and a real and lasting union of purpose effected. Had they believed these things at the very moment of their revolution and had they been confirmed in that belief since, the sad reverses which have recently marked the progress of their affairs toward an ordered and stable government of free men might have been avoided.

The question in 1917-18 was just as unanswerable as it is today: Who and how was anybody to arouse "sympathy and enthusiasm," to sweep away "suspicion and distrust" from a people utterly uninformed and lacking even practice of workable organization?

Colonel Thompson's memorandum to the President covered practically the same ground that Mr. Lloyd George had gone over in our discussions with him in London. It explained that William Boyce Thompson had just returned via London from Petrograd, having spent four months there in close touch with almost all elements of the situation. Colonel Thompson, under the general approval of Mr. Creel, the Administration's Director of Publicity, carried on certain educational work in Russia, designed (a) to acquaint the Russian people with the evil aims of German autocracy, and (b) to demonstrate the fundamental sympathy of America and of her Allies with the aspirations of the new Russia. Thompson's opinion, based upon the results of his work and upon his general observations in Russia, and also akin to the opinions expressed by Mr. Lloyd George and by Senator Root months before, was roughly as follows:

No matter how hopeless the situation looks, it is still well worth while to make a distinct effort to keep the Germans from dominating the Russian situation. Russia as a fighting force may well be gone, but if the Allies handle the situation wisely and vigorously they can still maintain it as a menace to Germany. The Germans have made rapid strides in getting hold of the Russian situation, employing all sorts of methods, corrupt and otherwise, in the attempt to render the dominating elements (shifting from day to day) their own. Germany is now making her most vigorous attempts with the Bolsheviks.

The Allies have either openly or secretly tried to bring back elements of the old order, or else they have failed to try to keep on friendly terms with the newer ruling elements, whatever they might be. The British Military Attaché, as Mr. Lloyd George has said, made a very bad break, in helping to get rid of Kerensky, who at least was the firm friend of the Allies, and opposed to a separate peace.

It should be well understood that a complete reorientation of parties has taken place. The Milyukoffs, etc., who were the leaders in deposing the Czar (April, 1917) now have moved over to the extreme Right, the elements formerly represented by Kerensky now forming the Center.

The memorandum for the President went on:

Recognition of the Bolsheviks is not essential. Contact is. This contact, gained informally and unofficially, permits the changing situation to be followed exactly, and not by guess-work. At the same time it does not bind the Government in any degree. This committee would deal with conditions. It

93

would work through any and every group in the attempt to arouse Russia to the German menace.

The memorandum stressed the importance, just as Senator Root had done months before, of taking measures of practical relief — "a flow of supplies, exclusive of munitions, should be started to Russia at once. Such supplies *have been purchased* and are now under control of the Russian Embassy here. Let the Red Cross be asked to become agents for the distribution of them in Russia." The committee formation that Thompson advocated was the same as the small informal mission that the British Minister had suggested — made up perhaps simply of one representative each, appointed by Mr. Lloyd George and President Wilson. Thompson had planned to develop Mr. Lloyd George's idea further in his anticipated talk with the President.

The Wilson Administration had lost a trick in paying little heed to what was happening in those momentous weeks in Russia from December, 1917, through that final dismaying signing of the Brest-Litovsk Treaty on February 18th, 1918. Having turned a deaf ear to all appeals for sympathy and aid against what Germany was threatening and having let the whole issue go by the board, all we did when the Treaty was finally signed was to issue statements condemning in round terms the Soviet Government for having yielded to Germany's armed compulsion. We sent no aid, we gave no cooperation. We contented ourselves with words — fine words and then recriminations.

Matters went from bad to worse. The Allies allowed themselves to be persuaded that the Bolshevik movement was a flash in the pan and could readily be suppressed. So in April, 1918, America joined in with Britain, France and Japan in the misguided enterprise of invading Russia, under the sponsorship of some of the old Czarist generals, Kolchak, Denikin and others, and trying to subdue to their will 170 million people, badly led to be sure but always ready to defend the fatherland from foreign invasion.

Of all the essays that sober statesmen have ever been guilty of, that of attempting in the spring of 1918 to overturn the Soviet Government (which by that time had control over vast millions of Russians and of the regions that they occupied) was, as we look back, the maddest. Evidently, the French and British purely military authorities, and the Americans hardly less, were dead set on Russian intervention and apparently forced reluctant assents to the plan from Lord Balfour, Britain's Foreign Minister, and from President Wilson himself. The expedition was in every sense a disaster—not merely from the military rebuff and loss of repute that it gave to the Allies, but of far greater importance, because throughout the thirty years which have elapsed, that Allied attempt to rule Russia's internal affairs has continued to embitter the relations between Russia and the Western nations.

While Thompson and I were being refused audience at the White House in late December, 1917, and early 1918, Mr. Lloyd George, tired of waiting, decided to act on his own and try out the method of contact with the Soviet Government. He sent out as diplomatic agent Bruce Lockhart, a canny Scotsman who, badly handicapped by the absence of an American associate — for the Soviet Government was highly suspicious of British intentions — quickly made his presence known. The Soviets expressed satisfaction in Britain's interest, but Britain was in no position to render even the limited aid that America, in Russia's then desperate plight, could. Bruce Lockhart had a young, vigorous personality. But he had nothing very tangible to offer and could accomplish little.

Not many years ago, reviewing the whole episode with him, I asked him the specific question as to whether if Mr. Lloyd George's plan had gone smoothly and if President Wilson had been willing to listen to the situation and join in a limited attempt to meet it, the course of history would have been changed at all. I expressed my own view that in no event did we ever have knowledge that Lenin and Trotsky would act in good faith and that, even with a joint Anglo-American Mission on the scene, Lenin and Trotsky would have been unable to withstand Germany's pressure to compel them to sign the Brest-Litovsk Treaty on the dotted line.

Bruce Lockhart was inclined to agree. But, said he, if President Wilson had sent a first-class man to join him he believed the two would have been able to accomplish one thing that over the years would have proved of the greatest importance in preventing the deterioration of relations between the Soviets on the one hand and America and Britain on the other. According to his argument, our joint mission would have been able to prevent the 1918 invasion of Russia by the Allies which, ever since that time, has been the greatest source of suspicion to the Soviet Government and to the Russian people, and is today one of the chief factors that continues to make relations difficult.

As I look back upon American relations with Russia over those two years of 1917 and 1918, I try to shrug my shoulders and be philosophical enough to say: "Oh, well, even had American failures, American mistakes not been made, nevertheless in the long run the results of our attitude towards Russia would have been unchanged and the Bolsheviks would have pursued the selfsame course. Prompt action upon the Root Mission Report or upon Lloyd George's proposal to Thompson and me, even if the President had allowed himself to listen to it — such action would not have changed the mighty sweep of events that have carried us to some of our lamentable, present-day impasses with the Soviets."

And yet the still, small voice of Marshal Zhukoff comes harking back to my ears. The story may be apocryphal. It is of a conversation in Germany in 1945 between General Eisenhower and Marshal Zhukoff. "Marshal," said the American general, "you know America has no designs against your people. You must not be so suspicious of us." To which the Marshal replied: "For more than twenty years we have taught our soldiers and our people to be suspicious. It will take the same time to learn not to suspect others."

11

VENTURE IN PUBLISHING

In the early autumn of 1918
I bought the *New York Evening Post* from Oswald
Garrison Villard, whom I had known since my college
days at Harvard; and it was especially in this connection
that President Wilson invited me to see him at the White
House early in October. We talked first about the
Evening Post. I told the President that, as already announced, I had divorced myself from the management
of the property, having placed all the shares in a completely independent trust, the trustees being Dr. Henry
S. Pritchett, of The Carnegie Foundation for the Advancement of Teaching, Theodore N. Vail, the head
of the American Telephone and Telegraph Company,
one of the great and wise figures in the business world,
and Ellery Sedgwick, editor of *The Atlantic Monthly*,
an old-time college friend.

I took this step of course to head off any gossip that I
intended to run the newspaper for the benefit of any
special interests, financial or other. I wished the editors
to feel under no possible obligation to be guided by my
views or even to seek them. And indeed, I kept my
hands strictly off any attempt to dictate the journal's

policies; but I did express to the Editor, the late Rollo Ogden, the hope that the *Evening Post* would see its way clear to support completely the idea of the League of Nations. That I found was already the purpose of the editors.

I further explained to the President that I had been a life-long Republican, but that like almost every other American I was wholeheartedly for his war policy, and I intended to do everything in my power to support his scheme for a world peace organization. At that time the title "League of Nations" had not yet been given to it.

Mr. Wilson responded cordially. Then he told me of his plan, not yet announced, to make public appeal for the return of a Democratic Congress at the approaching November 5th election. I asked him what class of voter he expected to gain by his announcement that would not in any event vote the Democratic ticket. "The independent vote," was the President's reply. I said that I could readily see the reason for his desire — like Abraham Lincoln he did not want "a house divided." But I thought he would do better if he rested upon his outstanding war record and let that speak for him and for his party. His choice of General Pershing as commander of the American Expeditionary Forces in France, his superb handling of our soldiers, their marvellous gallantry and successes, the outstanding record of Newton D. Baker, Secretary of War — all these factors counted heavily with the American people in the President's favor.

I went on to say that a public appeal would perhaps be taken as a sign of weakness. The President pleasantly disagreed and we let it go at that. Needless to recall, the Congressional elections went decisively Republican. Even, however, with this portent so threatening in the political skies, the President seemingly modified in no way the drafting of the League of Nations Covenant.

In purchasing the *Evening Post*, I was moved by various considerations, partly sentimental. My elder brother Hammond Lamont, for whom I had the most tender memory, had years before been Managing Editor of the *Evening Post*, and at the time of his death in 1909 was Editor of the weekly then associated with it, *The Nation*. My sister's husband, John P. Gavit, had likewise been the *Evening Post's* Managing Editor. A greater consideration, however, was the fear expressed in many journalistic quarters that, if the owner, Mr. Villard, felt it essential to press a sale, this newspaper property, its high repute dating back to the time of Alexander Hamilton, might fall into hands less desirable than those of its former owners. The chief factor, however, that led me to make the purchase was, I think, the hankering that in my four early years in journalism I had gained for further essay in the newspaper field. I rather imagined myself gradually withdrawing from various affairs and giving myself over to the possible fulfillment of early dreams.

Fate, however, decreed quite otherwise. World War I had increased enormously the business activities and public responsibilities of myself and all my associates in the Morgan firm. Very likely I should not in any event have felt myself free to drop the pressing affairs in which, with my partners, I was engaged. But the question was really settled for me by the fatal illness in 1922 of my beloved friend and partner, Harry Davison, who early in 1917 had withdrawn completely from the Morgan firm's affairs and devoted his energies, even to the end of his life, to the work of rehabilitating and expanding enormously the activities of the American Red Cross. A superb leader and organizer himself, Davison changed the Red Cross from a local Washington affair into an enterprise in which the whole American people took part.

Prior even to Davison's early and lamented death, I had been obliged to absent myself on long official or semi-official missions, as described elsewhere in this narration. The consequence of these absences and diversions was that I paid not the slightest heed to the affairs of the *Evening Post,* and in a financial way it went from the difficult days of the Villard regime to the worst that I could imagine. Frank A. Munsey, an exceedingly active and competent newspaper publisher whom I liked but with whose ideas I did not altogether agree, was nothing if not ambitious. He invited himself down to 23 Wall Street for luncheon with me. Whereupon followed an episode in connection with the *Evening Post* in which I take some pride.

Frank Munsey was brief and to the point. "What did you pay for the property — $1,000,000?"

"Yes."

"What did you lose the first year, Tom?"

"$700,000."

"Then you are $1,700,000 out of pocket. I will give you $1,700,000 tomorrow morning for the property."

This was an immensely handsome offer, but I was uneasy. "What will you plan to do with the property, Frank?"

"Scrap it at once. Save the AP franchise for one of my other papers, and let it go at that."

"Well," I said, "I am terribly sorry that I can't take advantage of your offer. It is a generous one, but I cannot bear to see an old property like that deliberately thrown down the drain. I think I will stick it out for a while."

Certainly the property was far too great a luxury for me to indulge in. But I could not bear to think of oblivion for a journal that, even though at times unduly pedantic and querulous, had been such a power for righteousness in the land. So at their earnest solicitation I sold the property on a shoe string to the group that was editing and publishing it, headed by Edwin F. Gay, founder and first head of the Harvard School of Business Administration, a man of outstanding character and ability but entirely inexperienced in the newspaper field. But the ship could not be kept off the rocks.

So next it was the late Cyrus H. K. Curtis, publisher of the *Saturday Evening Post* of Philadelphia and kindred periodicals, also of the *Philadelphia Public Ledger*, that asked to come to luncheon. Said Mr. Curtis, with whom for years I had enjoyed friendly acquaintance: "Mr. Lamont, I need a financial editor for the *Public Ledger* badly. Where can I get one?"

"The best one I know," I replied, "is the financial editor of *The New York Evening Post*, Franz Schneider, Jr. But I don't think you can get him."

"Could I get him if I took over the property as well?" asked Mr. Curtis, simply voicing the thought that I believe had always been uppermost in his mind.

So we made the deal then and there. Mr. Curtis was far less lavish and more businesslike than Mr. Munsey had been. He certainly planned to continue and manage the property, and he assured me that he intended to preserve the high traditions that I cherished for it. Money-wise I should have been better off, by many hundreds of thousands of dollars, to have accepted Mr. Munsey's offer, yet at least I could sleep with an easy conscience as to my duty to the *Evening Post*.

III

The Peace Conference

12

PARIS PEACE CONFERENCE

The Paris Peace Conference lasted from mid-January, 1919, until the end of June when the Treaty was signed. I arrived at Paris the first week in February. The Secretary of the Treasury, Carter Glass, had designated the late Norman H. Davis and me as the representatives of the United States Treasury on the American Commission. From the time of my arrival until my return with President Wilson on the *George Washington* on June 30, my days and many nights were filled with the activities of the Peace Conference, culminating with the impressive ceremony of the Treaty signing at Versailles on June 28th.

I chanced to have had considerable acquaintance with some of the British and French leaders and was drawn into various phases of the treaty-making. But my chief preoccupation was with the harassing and ever present subject of German reparations. As an active American representative on the Sub-Committee to determine Germany's capacity and means of payment, I was called upon to draft various clauses of the treaty that bore upon the subject. Throughout the Conference I, like my immediate associates, Norman H. Davis, Vance

McCormick, and Bernard M. Baruch, was called into frequent consultation with the Big Four — President Wilson, Prime Minister Lloyd George, Premier Clemenceau, and Premier Orlando of Italy.

These chapters are not intended as another of the many histories of the Paris Conference. Rather they are designed to give a picture of various phases of the work there, an account of the moods and tenses of the various delegations; to touch upon some of the chief personalities; to recite some of the whys and wherefores that brought about certain results; and, finally, to describe the struggle over the ever-pressing subject of reparations. The world of today and all the mighty events that are passing before us are of infinitely greater interest to me than the happenings of yesterday. Yet it is my hope that in recounting certain phases of the Conference of 1919, I may be able to throw some little light upon our struggles in the post-war world of today.

One must remember the confusion of mind and circumstance amid which the Peace conferees had to work. The delegates were distracted by a thousand immediate troubles left in the wake of the vast and disastrous conflict that had been waged. First of all were hunger and other distressing conditions on the Continent that called for immediate relief. In some countries a lively inflation was well under way. There was the constant threat of Bolshevism (undoubtedly grossly exaggerated by the Germans for political purposes). Then there was the fateful dissolution of the old Austro-Hungarian Empire, that great area of free trade that had helped to stabilize all Europe.

Almost thirty different nations, old and new, were emerging from the maelstrom caused by the break-up of Europe. Most of them, in the course of our deliberations in 1919, were already busy, setting up new nationalistic policies, including trade barriers. Representatives from all these old and new European nationalities, as well as representatives from many non-European powers, had posted off to Paris and were sitting there day by day, urging their claims upon the peace-makers and occupying in sum total an immense amount of their time. I can hardly exaggerate the bedlam let loose when all these individuals and contingents crowded into Paris and hurled themselves upon the already sorely beset peace-makers.

Thus the Allied delegations had to cope with existing conditions, and at the same time set up a treaty that would pave the way for a peaceful new world. Not only were they trying to right the wrongs that had been committed, but in many instances they were endeavoring to carry out contradictory policies. For example, just as today, the Allies felt that they must build up Germany to a point where she was capable of producing revenues available for her own support and for the payment of adequate reparations. On the other hand, she must not become so renewed and strengthened as to turn into a later war threat or into too great a trade rival.

On top of all this there had to be created, according to President Wilson, a new mechanism that would preserve the world from future conflict. Britain and France, aware of the state of Europe and knowing that early progress in the peace-making was essential, preferred that the organization of the League of Nations be post-poned until after the work on the other parts of the Treaty had got well under way. But President Wilson put his foot down on that, and that was all there was to it. I have argued to myself that this priority of the Covenant, insisted upon by the President, did not delay unduly the Peace Treaty itself. But I confess I was never perfectly clear in my own mind about it. Certainly Mr. Wilson was able to take no real working interest in the pressing and desperately important problems of terri-torial, reparations, colonial, and other settlements, until the Covenant had long been drafted and was made public.

Most of us Americans failed to realize fully enough the terrific sufferings that the two chief Allies had under-gone. We did not overlook, but yet made insufficient allowance for, the frightful loss of young life that had fallen upon them, the destruction of industries, towns and countryside, the deadly war weariness that dragged them down. It was in World War II that I heard an American returning from a blitzed and devastated Lon-don say that no American safe and secure from direct enemy fire could possibly appreciate what the British people were undergoing; whereupon an Englishman present declared, "And none of us in England can ap-preciate the desperate terror, degradation and torture to which the conquered countries on the Continent are subjected." So it was that we Americans in 1919 should, perhaps, have been somewhat more tolerant of the ten-sions under which the other representatives labored.

The chief treaty-makers at Paris were also constantly

handicapped by politics at home. The very democracies that Mr. Wilson had declared we were fighting "to make the world safe for" were frequently so vociferous that they prevented the leaders of states at Paris from always exercising their best judgment. In March, 1919, for example, in the midst of the discussions on reparations when we were considering the immediate assessment upon Germany of a fixed sum, Mr. Lloyd George readily admitted that such a course was in itself the wisest thing to do. Yet he finally refused to agree to it on the ground that the British public would be so furious with the greatly reduced figure demanded from Germany that it would throw out his Government. When the reparations crisis was at its height, Mr. Wilson asked Bernard Baruch and me to go and make a final plea to Mr. Lloyd George to agree to the naming of a fixed sum. We did so, and at the end of our argument he shook his head and said, "Well, Lamont, 'almost thou persuadest me' — you are right and I shall probably have to come over to your side." Just then, however, Mr. Bonar Law, one of his Ministers, flew in from London and told him of a fresh outbreak in the House of Commons for newer and higher demands against Germany. Whereupon Mr. Lloyd George threw up the sponge and said the jig was up as to any fixed sum for reparations.

Clemenceau's position was of much the same kind. Neither of these chiefs of state felt himself free to decide on the naming at once of a specific sum that Germany must pay, fearing that their respective democracies would be so dissatisfied with the amount of it that they would toss them out of office. President Wilson had also an American democracy to deal with. Unhappily he proved unable to handle it or its representatives in the United States Senate. Hence the tragedy of the League of Nations that I shall reserve for another chapter.

Wilson was such a believer in the soundness of the people, that he acted upon the idea that he could appeal successfully to them over the heads of their rulers. An outstanding example of this was the case of Fiume when the Italian Prime Minister refused to relinquish Italy's claim to this strategic city. It may be worth while to tell of this in some detail:

President Wilson had swallowed Italy's claim to the Trentino. That lovely upland region of the Dolomites, for generations shepherded by the South Austrians, would never have been promised to Italy at London in 1915, had it not been the one prize that tipped the scales to get Italy to enter the war on the Allied side against Austria (1915) and Germany (1916).

When, however, it came to the port of Fiume, at the head of the Adriatic, President Wilson gagged. He had swallowed the Trentino camel, but in the process he had acquired such a distaste for gnats that he closed his lips sternly against Fiume. He stood by the newly created Yugoslavia's claim to the port. Meanwhile, however, the poet-militarist, d'Annunzio, at the head of a band of volunteers seized Fiume. Thereupon the imagination of the whole Italian people flared up and d'Annunzio at once became Italy's hero. It was made clear to Orlando that if he gave in he would, upon his return to Italy, be ousted from office or something worse. He just could not give way.

But President Wilson, feeling he had yielded too much in the Trentino matter which had been much less exploited, would not budge an inch on Fiume. At the afternoon meeting of the Big Four on April 23, 1919, he did not state just what he planned to do, but his attitude was obdurate, and it was easy for us to see that Orlando was in a blue funk. Lloyd George and Clemenceau tried some sweet reasonableness, but Mr. Wilson would have none of it. And Orlando's plea that the Wilson solution would oust him from office and compel Italy to withdraw from the Conference fell on deaf ears.

On the following morning I received a summons from President Wilson to wait on him at his home. When I entered his study I found the President down on his hands and knees on the floor, studying a large-scale map of Italy, the Adriatic, and so on. As he rose and greeted me he declared that the Fiume situation was just as he had thought. Fiume, he explained, had been a part of Hungary for centuries, and as that region of the broken Austro-Hungarian Empire was now Yugoslavian, Fiume could not be awarded to Italy.

In reply to my respectful inquiry as to his possible plan of action, the President explained that his proper course seemed clear to him: he would tell the Italian people, just as he had tried to make their Premier understand, that they had no rights in Fiume and would no doubt, in the interests of harmony, wish to give up their claims. When I mentioned what Orlando had stressed in the previous day's session, namely, that there was a great outcry in the Italian public press over Fiume and that an about-face would be impossible, the President said, "Ah, Lamont, you do not understand. In every civilized people there is a latent sense of justice that has only to be appealed to in order to assert itself."

Mr. Wilson added that in fact he had already given out for the afternoon press his decision and a copy of his appeal made to the Italian people over the heads of their rulers.

The result was just the opposite of what Mr. Wilson had expected. Mobs formed in Italian cities, shrieking against President Wilson's appeal. Premier Orlando and his delegation left the Conference in a huff and went back to Rome. For the time being this unstudied action of the President's had precipitated a major crisis in the procedure of the Conference.

In fact Japan, who had fought on the Allied side, seized upon this as the psychological moment to make good her claim that all the extensive rights, political and otherwise, that Germany had acquired some years before in the Chinese province of Shantung, should be transferred to Japan. President Wilson, confronted with the possibility that a refusal might result in Japan's withdrawal from the Peace Conference, yielded, though with great anguish of spirit, to the Japanese demands.

Ray Stannard Baker, in his *American Chronicle*, says that on one occasion in Paris he was arguing with the President about the proposed concession to Japan on Shantung. According to Baker, this colloquy then ensued: "The opinion of the world," said Baker, "supports the Chinese claims." "I know that," replied the President. "Especially American public opinion," added Baker. "I know that, too," responded Mr. Wilson, "but if the Italians remain away and the Japanese go home, what becomes of the League of Nations?"

Wilson considered that the Shantung settlement was the severest compromise that we had been obliged to make, and he made it only after saying again and again to the Japs that the settlement must not mean any exploitation of China by Japan or the closing of the Open Door. He was in hopes that all special spheres of influence in China could be abandoned after a while.

The 1915-1916 treaties—the so-called Secret Treaties — under which Italy had been brought into the war on the side of the Allies, and on which Japan based her claim to the German rights in Shantung, were an additional factor which complicated the peace-making. Lloyd George and Clemenceau had to do as best they could in the war of compromises with the signatory governments. I remember hearing President Wilson once remark that the other premiers were astonishingly frank in describing their difficulties. For instance, Lloyd George once said to him that the treaty with Italy in 1915 would never have been executed if Lord Grey, Britain's Foreign Minister, had been on his feet. But Asquith, then Prime Minister, did it all by himself and then brought it in to the Cabinet as a *fait accompli*. When they read it the whole British Cabinet threw up their hands in despair. But Asquith said that Italy had named her price for entering the war and he had had to pay it. Lloyd George was bitter against Asquith for giving way.

America's Allies were also greatly bothered by the existence of the Fourteen Points. Early in 1918 President Wilson had set forth in the Fourteen Points what

he saw as the chief requirements that Germany would
have to meet in order to bring about a peace. Some of
the Fourteen Points were specific, others were vague.
They were hurriedly put together, and on none of them
had Wilson consulted the other chiefs of state. Most of
the Fourteen Points had admirable features, but, being
written without long deliberation, some of them though
sounding good were unworkable.

The Germans always claimed that not only the Armistice of November 11, 1918, but the peace itself, must
be based solely on the Fourteen Points. They set up the
claim that they were simply making peace on the basis of
the Fourteen Points and that they had never been defeated. Despite the defeat and surrender of the German
armies, navy, and the nation itself, this attitude of theirs
made headway with the public in both Britain and
America.

T. E. Jessop, the distinguished professor of philosophy in the University College of Hull, in his small but
illuminating volume called *The Treaty of Versailles —
Was It Just?* says that an experienced diplomat who had
represented Germany in Washington until its rupture
with the United States in 1917 later stated: "A legend
has been fostered in Germany to the effect that we laid
down our weapons in reliance on the Fourteen Points.
This legend is a flat falsification of history as everyone
knew who then took part in the negotiations. We had to
lay down our arms because the Supreme Army Command insisted that we should do so in order to avoid a
catastrophe, and then we invoked Wilson's help, with an
appeal to the Fourteen Points. . . . His intervention was

of advantage to us, for we thus acquired a moral right. The Peace of Versailles thus became the breach of an undertaking when it would otherwise have merely been the consequence of our military defeat." This from a high German official!

Among other points President Wilson laid great emphasis on the principle of "self-determination," that is to say, there should be no state or even any extensive region to be ruled by a government other than that which the local population might elect as its representative. "Self-determination," Senator Root remarked back in 1920, "is a phrase that sounds too well. It symbolizes one of the several half-truths from which the world is now suffering. There is no absolute right of self-determination, either in morals or in reason. It must always be conditioned. For example, the right of self-determination, if absolute and granted, would create a German enclave in Wisconsin."

As a corollary to the principle of universal democracy for which Woodrow Wilson was giving his life, his urge for "self-determination" by national groups was natural. Yet it was because he interpreted that concept too literally and too sweepingly that he and the other members of the Big Four, with equal or greater responsibility, reached decisions in Eastern Europe, especially in the final break-up of the old Austro-Hungarian Empire, that were destined in the post-war years to weaken enormously the entire structure of the European economy.

Another weakness of the Versailles Treaty was due to that sublime faith that President Wilson put in a reformed, democratic Germany. So passionate was Wood-

row Wilson's faith in democracy as the remedy for all
political ills, that it was apparently impossible for him to
conceive of groups of men who, given the chance,
would not leap forward to grasp the talisman that would
cure and make them whole. Throughout and following
World War I he conceived of Germany as made up of
people longing to be set free from the bonds of state
worship and military tradition, and yearning to establish
a thoroughly democratic state. In one of his pre-Armi-
stice speeches he had said we had not been warring on
the German people, but on their rulers. In 1918 he had
refused to enter into an armistice with a Germany that
still clung to a monarchy. In his first exchange of Armistice notes with Germany in October, 1918, he insisted
that the regime of the Hohenzollerns (under whom, bad
as they were, there had been maintained a stable rule)
should be thrown out of the window and a republic of
the people substituted for it.

With all his study of history President Wilson failed
to understand the traditions and character of the German people. And his belief that a thoroughly democratic Germany could readily spring into being was
pretty generally shared by the American people and
certainly by our delegation at Paris.

That idea of Germany was a grave misconception.
The German people had never shown signs of democratic tendencies and certainly no desire to struggle for
the faith. Just after World War I they were in the same
mood as they are today, though under far less wretched
conditions than now prevail in the large cities. Now,
too, according to all trustworthy reports, there is little

evidence that the Germans have been won to the democratic way of life, and virtually none that they have learned that war does not pay. They are sorry for themselves, but they are not remorseful about anything, save, perhaps, that they lost the war — "better luck next time."

There is one striking difference between the situation as to Germany confronting the Allies today and that facing them at the end of World War I. Then Germany, although its modern history had been marked by certain breaches of treaties and unprovoked aggressions, was still considered to be a civilized nation which must be treated in the peace on certain hypotheses. The first hypothesis was that her material rebuilding was essential to the economy of the Continent as a whole; second that she would so comport herself as shortly to qualify to take her place again in the community of nations. In 1919 there could be no such realization as there is now that we were but at the end of the first part of another Thirty Years (1914-1944) war; that Germany under the Prussian leaders, always arrogant and imbued with the theory of the Herrenvolk and of national supremacy, was, in the absence of rigid supervision, likely to break out again into armed conflict, waged with increased ferocity and cruelty.

At Paris, Mr. Wilson was, as I have said, a firm believer in the idea that, given the chance, peoples would eagerly turn themselves almost overnight from totalitarianism to democracy. Clemenceau, on the other hand, being convinced of the complete absence of any truly democratic element in Germany, said so frequently. It was his belief that democracy was a matter of conviction and tradition; that it could not be made to work overnight. He was completely disillusioned as to there being any real basis of good will or democratic purpose in Germany. And while he hoped it might come true, the Wilsonian phrase that "We are fighting this war to end all wars" seemed to him chimerical. Although to the President, in those long afternoon sessions in Mr. Wilson's library, M. Clemenceau was always most courteous, there could never be any doubt of his opinion of certain of the President's utterances, including in fact a good part of the Fourteen Points.

Clemenceau was convinced that Germany, especially Prussia, never could at any time in any way be trusted, and this was the burden of his song from day to day until both the President and Mr. Lloyd George became impatient of it. Both of them believed in a future Germany that would be well behaved — the President because he thought she could readily be turned into a purely democratic state, Mr. Lloyd George because Germany had for years been Britain's best trade customer, and he was determined to retain her valuable trade for Britain.

As Clemenceau sat there ruminating about Italy, about the Balkan countries, and very particularly about Germany, the idea of making a world "safe for democracy" had little appeal for him. He knew it would take years, perhaps generations, for those countries to work into such a form of government. He insisted that Germany did not have the first element of democracy within its borders. He was right. Neither the leopards nor the Germans change their spots.

13

THE SETTLEMENT WITH GERMANY

When President Wilson arrived in Europe in mid-December, 1918, the welcome that he received in every country from government and people alike was overwhelming. That moment of his landing and reception in Europe marked the zenith of his power. He was the statesman who, by his adroit correspondence, had induced Austria-Hungary to abandon her German ally and to make an earlier surrender. He it was who had conducted by himself the negotiations that ended in the Armistice with Germany on November 11th.

The welcome given Wilson was so fervent that it inevitably gave the American President the feeling that the whole world, including his own country, must be in accord with his views. It was to a considerable extent this feeling that the whole Allied world was for him that led to his conviction that nobody could be against him, and especially that his own country would never reject his particular construction of the League Covenant.

The organization of global peace and the attainment of world-wide democracy were the two ideals that ruled Mr. Wilson's mind and his political life. They were such an obsession with him as not infrequently to blind him as to method and a sense of timing. Thus in the field of accomplishment he often failed. But his failures were always of the mind, never of the heart. What in the record may well sound like criticism, must always be far more than offset by the pride of the American people that they were able to produce a leader of such idealism and unswerving purpose.

President Wilson, despite his failures, was the outstanding figure of the Peace Conference. His intervention not only for the immediate establishment of a League of Nations, but in many important questions that were strictly European, was commanding. Unless my guess fails, history will preserve for Woodrow Wilson — for that lofty idealism and that indomitable will of his — a niche that will remain long after the figures of Lloyd George and Clemenceau have faded away into misty legend.

President Wilson had the devotion of his own delegation to a man, but from the start he and his delegation had a certain handicap which was inherent in the situation. That was lack of day-by-day experience in foreign affairs. The Americans were strong for the idealistic ends that they worked for, but they could not know from previous experience how many of them were in world affairs workable or unworkable. In point of ability, character and learning the American delegation had high repute, made up of experts like Charles Seymour of Yale and Archibald Coolidge of Harvard in history, Isaiah Bowman, now of Johns Hopkins, in political geography, Allyn Young of Cornell in economics, and various others that I could name who did superb work in their fields.

On the other hand, the British and French, not to speak of all the minor delegations, came to the Conference well equipped and with a pretty clear knowledge of what they intended to work for. France, after her first end, which must be security from Germany, required as much reparations as she could possibly obtain. This was a reasonable attitude, because of the vast material damage that Germany had inflicted upon northern France, the destruction of her coal mines, and a thousand other acts of demolition. In addition was the fact that the death and maiming of her younger generation on the field of battle had so wounded and bled the whole nation that it was bound to be weakened for generations to come.

Britain, too, had a pretty clear idea of the end she should attain. For generations Britain had maintained the balance of power on the Continent of Europe, and this "balance of power," instead of being the deplorable thing that so many people seem to think, was the set-up that most served to maintain world peace for one hundred years following the Congress of Vienna in 1815. Britain therefore wished no one continental nation to be unduly weakened or unduly strengthened.

Britain believed it prudent that Germany, with her war powers curbed, should be maintained as the leading industrial and trading nation of Central Europe. With this President Wilson agreed. He and Mr. Lloyd George felt that Germany was the economic backbone of Europe, that her industry and trade were absolute necessities for the well-being of the rest of the Continent. That, plus the necessity that Germany's subsistence should not continually remain as a burden upon the Allies, is of course precisely the same argument for the reindustrialization of Germany being heard today after World War II.

German recovery could not be accomplished, however, without strengthening Germany economically to a point that to the French seemed highly dangerous to their own economy and safety, as in fact it was. But the British were inclined to pooh-pooh France's fear of further invasion. As for reparations, Britain wanted as large a sum as she could possibly obtain that could be transferred from the mark into other currencies. She did not, however, in her desire for reparations, welcome a development that would see German manufactures exported and sold so cheaply that they served to cut severely into Britain's own export trade.

Beginning with the early days of the Conference, many of the British and Americans, for some reason that I could not readily fathom, seemed to be thoroughly impatient with the French, talking of their avariciousness, of their having no real aim for a just or ideal peace. Both delegations, including Mr. Lloyd George and President Wilson, became even annoyed by the repeated warnings of Premier Clemenceau on the subject of French security. Yet those pleas were the most natural thing in the world.

Clemenceau had been an eager young man in 1870 when Germany invaded and conquered France. He had seen his beloved country ruthlessly overrun by the Germans. He had, he believed, learned through and through what the Germans were like. With all this still vivid in his memory, and with the unprovoked invasion of August, 1914, what aim could he and his delegation have except security for France?

But the British and American delegations said in effect: "Oh, yes, that is all true, but Germany of course will never attack France again. She has been too hard hit by this defeat. You French are worrying over nothing. Sit down with us now and help us work out a peace that will re-establish Germany's industry, and get her going, so that she can play her important role as the leading industrial and commercial state of Europe."

"Won't you make a visit with us to the devastated regions of France, so that you can see for yourself what the Germans have done to us?" begged M. Clemenceau of President Wilson. Mr. Wilson's reply, perhaps not unnaturally, was that he was too much pressed to do that; he would have to wait until later. According to one report he added that he did not want his cool judgment blurred by the sight of devastation and suffering. The French were begging that their milch cows and other livestock that Germany had stolen from them and driven off to the Reich be restored. This plea, as I put down in my brief diary at the time, annoyed Mr. Wilson. He wanted to know how in the world the French could go into Germany and pick out the cattle that had been stolen from them. He said it was an impossible proposition.

Wilson and his associates, believing in the future effectiveness of the League of Nations with our own active

125

participation in it, told Clemenceau that in that way he would surely have his security. In fact, President Wilson was so in earnest about it that he was quite willing to sign a treaty with France that pledged American and British intervention in the event that France suffered another attack from Germany. But Mr. Clemenceau remained an unhappy man. He knew well enough that he had no assurance that the Tripartite Treaty of Defense would be ratified by the United States Senate. It was not ratified. It fell to rack and ruin with the main treaty, the League of Nations, and everything that went with it. And within the next decade France was to see the strong reconstruction of Germany through the aid largely of American and British capital, provided, to be sure, with the express approval of each of these two governments, and finally with the cooperation of the French Government itself.

As one looks back, especially one that was active on the Reparations Commission and in many of the conferences of the Big Four, it seems true enough that France's plea for security was hardly given the attention it deserved. If heeded, it would have benefited all the Allies.

We Anglo-Saxons proved ourselves a naive and trusting people at Versailles, and most of us continued in that attitude during the years between the wars. We were all more or less fooled by Germany from the start to the finish. The world found out in due course that Germany had set out on a deliberate campaign to evade her obligations. She succeeded beyond her wildest dreams. The German leaders adopted the policy of teaching their public so thoroughly that Germany could not pay repar-

ations, that the public came to believe it as they would
the gospel. You cannot expect a nation to make an effort
which its leaders declare is not possible of accomplishment.

From the very start of the peace discussions at Paris
the whole German public set up such a calamity cry as
to soften and fool at any rate the British and Americans,
even if not the French. The Germans complained bitterly that they were starving to death. No doubt some
of them were on exceedingly short rations. Yet to receive ample food supplies all they had to do was to carry
out what they had promised, namely, to turn over their
minor commercial shipping to the Allies. Because of the
German complaints the British press began to be filled
with letters expressing pity for the Germans, and begging
the Government to send them food in any event.*

The greatest other single factor in changing public
opinion on both sides of the water and in getting both
America and Britain to believe that the Versailles Treaty
constituted a hard and unjust burden for Germany, was
the stand taken by the brilliant John Maynard Keynes
in his famous book *The Economic Consequences of the
Peace*. This volume, published on a wide scale on both
sides of the Atlantic, soon became a Bible for all the
so-called liberals. In essence both Britain and America
became convinced that the Versailles Treaty generally
(although Keynes' book was based chiefly upon the
reparations clauses) was a cruel affair and not worth
standing by.

Since the outbreak of World War II, thinking people,

---

* I describe this episode fully in Chapter 15.

when they have given any consideration at all to the Versailles Treaty, have begun to realize that the trouble with the Versailles Treaty was not that it was too hard on Germany, even in its economic clauses. Rather, the chief difficulties were these:

First, the American delegation and many important, though perhaps junior, members of the British delegation had been so convinced that peace must be made strictly on the basis of President Wilson's Fourteen Points that they produced a peace that was more than just to Germany and less than just to the Allies.

Second, the Treaty was never enforced. From the date that it was signed, in fact almost from the beginning of the Armistice, the Germans began to welch on their promises and obligations. The greater were their breaches of faith over the following years, the more culpable were the Allies in condoning them and thus encouraging them to break their pledges further. Britain and America, in undertaking loans to Germany, believed that a restored Germany must be a happy Germany, and that a happy Germany could not possibly want war. In point of fact, they were helping to rejuvenate and strengthen Germany in her secret plans for a second attempt at conquest.

Third, in setting up the Versailles Treaty the Allies, with the exception of France and possibly Belgium, ignored the character of the Prussians with whom they were dealing. Most of us had never learned well our modern European history. We overlooked the fact that these precious Prussians had for generations been bred for armed aggression; that beginning under Bismarck's iron tutelage, they had learned thrice of the glories and the spoils of war, even before World War I. By their swift attacks successively on Denmark (1864), Austria (1866), and France (1870), they had raised themselves to the position of absolute rulers of a greatly enlarged Reich.

The Versailles Treaty was never enforced, and Germany's determination to disregard its most important provisions was realized without much difficulty. America rejected the Versailles Treaty because of her unwillingness to join the League of Nations on the exact terms that President Wilson had laid down, and entered into a separate peace with Germany preserving the difficult and troublesome features of the Versailles Treaty and losing the ameliorating conditions provided in the League Covenant. Following America's example of defection, Britain and France within two or three years began to split apart in their own counsels and policies as to handling Germany.

Germany's success in repudiation, right through to the time when Hitler came into power, unquestionably encouraged him to break the repeated pledges of non-aggression and comity that he and his predecessors as Chancellor had signed with the neighboring nations of Europe. Had the Allies enforced the much maligned Versailles Treaty, they could have repaired at least a modicum of the destruction suffered at the hands of Germany; they would have kept the Germans from rebuilding their war industries; they might have been able to prevent the Nazis under Hitler's leadership from plunging the world into the catastrophe of World War II.

Several generations having gone by since the death of liberalism in Germany, it is no wonder that for the Anglo-Saxon peoples and the countries of Western Europe it has become a burning question whether the old liberalism of pre-Bismarck Germany can ever be reanimated and made to live again, in politics, and in every other realm of human affairs and conduct.

14

THE QUESTION OF REPARATIONS

Mr. Norman Davis and I were the American representatives assigned to that phase of German reparations which had to do with Germany's capacity to pay. Our Sub-Committee No. 2, under the chairmanship of Lord Cunliffe, former Governor of the Bank of England, and vice-chairmanship of Louis Loucheur, a member of the French Cabinet, held scores of meetings between the date of convening and the signing of the Treaty. These gatherings were usually at the French Ministry of Finance at the lower end of the Rue de Rivoli. We met both morning and afternoon, and not infrequently evenings as well.

The question of reparations was highly controversial, and involved almost unending negotiation. There were constant ups and downs, almost daily storms, and sometimes hurricanes. In the whole course of the negotiations there was hardly a tranquil moment.

We got off to rather a bad start. Norman Davis and I had assumed that the British representatives and we would see eye to eye on the question of Germany's capacity to pay and transfer reparations. To our surprise and almost consternation, at the first meeting when

Lord Cunliffe asked the three governments their opinions, he himself supported by his colleague, Lord Sumner, came out with a figure equivalent at the rate of exchange in those days to $120 billion, which sounded fantastic. Indeed, this figure was surprising even to France. Lord Cunliffe had long been a personal friend of mine, and I had expected that at Paris we should surely agree on most things. But he and Lord Sumner were so certain of Germany's capacity to pay sky-high reparations that at the Conference everyone began to dub them "the heavenly twins."

Not to be outdone, however, by the British, M. Loucheur suggested, as a French estimate of Germany's capacity to pay, the equivalent of $200 billion, whispering to me that, after hearing what the British had to say, political considerations forced him up to that figure. Our American estimate was far less than either. Mr. Norman Davis thought a limit of approximately $30 billion was the extent that we ought to try for. I was somewhat more sanguine, feeling certain that the testimony of the Germans who had already begun to set up a wail about their possible burdens could not be relied upon. Knowing that their industrial plants had in no way been damaged, I thought that the equivalent of $40 billion could be managed.

From that initial point we began to go back over the whole ground and set up the data upon which our various estimates were based. Lord Cunliffe soon came down from his high horse to a figure equivalent to something like $57 billion, and the French followed suit. M. Loucheur told me privately that the French would be glad to abide by any figure which, in behalf of the American delegation, I felt was feasible.

It must be realized that although I speak primarily of the American, British and French delegations, representatives of the other nations that had been at war with Germany also had a part in these sessions, and even with the best will in the world, delayed and complicated them. Japan had little interest in cash reparations. She contented herself, as well she might, with having put in an unopposed claim for all the German-held islands in the Pacific north of the equator. She was in due course given a mandate over these, and in the following years handled them exclusively as her own, fortifying or utilizing them as bases as she desired, not, however, permitting visits to them by the people of other nations. The result of all this we found out to our cost in World War II, when the American Navy and our other armed forces had to force their way gradually, painfully, and bloodily through that whole fringe of islands until we could get within striking distance of the larger units like Okinawa where, after heavy loss of life and final capture, we could establish working bases against Japan.

It is difficult to give an adequate idea of the long-drawn-out procedure of these meetings of Sub-Committee No. 2 to determine Germany's capacity for payment. They were not open to the public. Nevertheless, each representative, especially of the smaller powers, felt himself obliged to make almost daily speeches for the benefit of his own associates and for the record that was distributed daily through the various delegations. We used to interrupt our afternoon sessions about four thirty o'clock and adjourn for a bit to one of the magnificent salons close at hand, where we were served with chocolate, whipped cream, and macaroons. These interruptions were welcome and often fruitful in enabling the delegates to exchange ideas informally and clear up by word of mouth many points of minor importance.

My particular *bête noir* at the Reparations sessions happened to be M. Klotz, French Minister of Finance, whose views were far less practicable than those of his colleague, M. Loucheur. With M. Klotz the American delegation was at constant war, and because it chanced that I was present at more meetings than some of the other Americans, engaged on other and equally important commissions, the brunt of battle with Klotz fell upon me. Klotz was thoroughly unreasonable. His own countrymen were against him. One afternoon, M. Clemenceau joined us all for our brief repast and asked me to sit down with him. He knew well of the passages at arms that I had had with his Minister of Finance and he whispered to me sepulchrally, "Be careful, Monsieur Lamont, Klotz will put poison in your chocolate!"

As the weeks slipped by the Belgians became exceedingly restless over the status of their claims against Germany: (a) reimbursement for war costs; (b) priority in claim as compared to the general reparations bill against Germany. While this matter occasioned no real crisis in the Conference, it became so troublesome that even this brief sketch should not omit mention of it.

Long before the end of the war, a priority in effect had been pledged to Belgium, because of Germany's gross breach of Belgium's neutrality, followed by ruthless invasion. Colonel House welcomed warmly the idea of especial consideration for Belgium and had a talk with Arthur J. Balfour (later the Earl of Balfour) who for the British delegation was equally in favor of the principle.

Then Norman Davis and I, at Colonel House's request, gave our attention to the matter and urged action by the Big Four. Mr. Lloyd George was, however, never in his most amiable mood with the Belgians. He grumbled a good deal over the idea of "war costs" for Belgium, whereas, for the Allies in general, at America's insistence, "war costs" had been eliminated from the category of claims that we might assess Germany. Eventually the Belgian delegation demanded a full-dress hearing before the Big Four, and they brought over their King to add his persuasions. A fine figure of a man, looking like a blonde Viking, he was rather pathetic in the manner in which he took my hand in both his own and thanked Mr. Davis and me for our efforts in behalf of his country.

At the meeting of the Big Four, Foreign Secretary Hymans made an appealing plea for Belgium, and finally Mr. Lloyd George, after a lot more complaining, moved that Loucheur of the French delegation and I should act as a committee to give the heads of state some formula for the Belgians that he could properly defend in the Commons.

Loucheur and I retired and before so very long returned with our formula which was far more the work of Loucheur's agile brain than my contribution. We recommended that Germany was to be obligated especially "to reimburse Belgium for all the sums borrowed from the Allies as a necessary consequence of the violation of the Treaty of 1839," in which Germany had joined Britian and France in pledging the neutrality of Belgium. Inasmuch as all such sums borrowed by Belgium were used for the prosecution of the war, this phrase was simply an euphemism for granting Belgium the war costs that she had demanded. But it was finally agreed to by all hands, and a crisis was averted. As a matter of fact, Germany herself repeatedly recognized her obligation to indemnify Belgium completely.

After weeks of hammering away to arrive at a figure that might reasonably represent Germany's capacity to pay, I was asked finally to draw up a recommendation for Sub-Committee No. 2 to make to the over-all Reparations Commission. If this were adopted, presumably the work of the Sub-Committee would be finished. I sat up a good part of the night in my rooms at the Meurice, writing out longhand this report, which in effect recommended as a task for the Germans a minimum figure of the equivalent of about $30 billion, and a maximum of the equivalent of about $40 billion.

Because of the vexing question of exchange, that is, the problem of how to transfer German marks into other currencies, I recommended that one-half of the total amount should be made payable in outside currencies to be designated by the Allies, the other half in marks within Germany which would then become the property of the Allies. This portion of reparations might take the form of liquid or static German assets. In either case it was presumed that the Allies would dispose of them gradually as the exchange markets proved able to stand the weight of them. Thus the matter would be cleared up eventually without too much of a burden on Germany. The constant endeavor of the American and British delegates was to make the Treaty conditions as workable as possible for Germany.

However, all our deliberations and our financial recommendations apparently were to go almost for naught, since M. Clemenceau and Mr. Lloyd George had both decided, as indicated heretofore, that the Sub-Committee's figure was so much less than their political constituencies had counted on that it must not be disclosed. We urged the President to take a firm stand in the naming of a present fixed sum. His invariable attitude, however, was that inasmuch as America claimed no share in reparations (except as to shipping), a matter of this kind must be left to the political discretion of the two Prime Ministers chiefly concerned.

When towards the end of May the Treaty had been transmitted to Germany and she was told she might make her own comments on it, Mr. Lloyd George, alarmed by the pro-Keynes storm gathering in England, fell into sort of a panic lest Germany should fail to sign the Treaty on the dotted line. He suddenly undertook to alleviate the terms, trying to make modifications, (1) in the eastern frontier, (2) in reparations, (3) as to the army of occupation, (4) as to admission to the League of Nations. The French would not for a moment accept any substantial changes, nor would Mr. Wilson for that matter.

This was just before the visit of the German representatives, invited to come and discuss the financial features of the document. The French would not allow the German delegates to come to the City of Paris, but insisted upon their staying at Senlis at the Château Villette, about an hour's motor drive from Paris. There we held several meetings. They had both their amusing and constructive sides. The German delegation included two German bankers of the Warburg firm whom I happened to know slightly and with whom I was glad to talk informally, for they seemed to be striving earnestly to offer some reparations composition that might be acceptable to the Allies. Count de Lasteraye, one of the French representatives, who prided himself upon his descent from Lafayette, and the contour of whose nose might well have confirmed his kinship, was fearful that some of us might say something to the Germans with which he was not in accord. He had a hard time keeping up with all the Allied delegates.

The German delegation finally made a suggestion which, if the heads of the Allied Governments had allowed us to consider it at the time, might have saved the world infinite difficulties. In these counter-proposals the Germans undertook to pay a total sum of 100 billion gold marks (the equivalent of \$25,000,000,000). This was subject to very considerable diminutions, and in no event could it have been accepted by the Allies without much dickering.

In the mood in which the Germans were then, and in view of the responsible German financiers who recommended the proposal, I think it quite possible that we might have secured what was in effect a voluntary commitment on the part of Germany to a sum equivalent of say $12 to $15 billion. Any settlement based on her own proposition would have been more difficult for Germany to evade, and a far higher total should ultimately have been collected than proved to be the case. The settlement which we could have traded out would have been at least equivalent to the amount, present value, which only two years later, Britain and France were glad to agree to, in the Paris settlement in February, 1921, between Mr. Lloyd George and M. Briand.

When, several weeks before, the determination had been reached that no fixed sum should be named as representing Germany's liability, then the proposal was brought forward for setting up a permanent Commission on Reparations. Mr. Lloyd George and M. Clemenceau both seized upon this suggestion rather eagerly, as forming a reasonable method by which they could postpone the final decision until the political horizon had cleared. At this time it was expected that America would, of course, sign the Treaty and would therefore have a place on the Commission. But this was not to be. Congress in a fitful expression of unwisdom refused President Wilson's plea that America should be represented upon the Commission. Yet Americans were after all destined to play an important part in the workings of the Commission.

My own belief is that the failure to name a fixed sum for the Germans to pay was the prime weakness that led to the interminable dragging out over the years of the whole problem of Reparations, and that led largely to the negation of the peace. We are aware that in any event Germany would have done her utmost by hook or crook to evade her payments, whatever they might have been; but in the undefined shape in which the whole reparations question was left at the time that the Treaty was signed at Versailles, it was a much simpler matter for the Germans further to confuse the reparations problem and to delay and evade payments under it.

From the signing of the Versailles Treaty in 1919 until Germany's final repudiation of all reparations payments twelve years later (even though the Allies had in the 1920s considerately supplied to her the bulk of the funds for making payment) there was constant and bitter economic warfare that thundered down the ways of all Europe, and affected even the seemingly remote Americas as well. Every country on the Continent suffered. Germany of course moaned and wailed constantly of her woes arising from reparations. Yet her worst troubles from start to finish were of her own making.

If we are generous to the Germans in our interpretation of the data, we arrive at the conclusion that Germany paid in reparations approximately 37 billion marks altogether, or the equivalent, let us say, of about $9 billion over a period of about fourteen years from 1918 to 1932, when her payments came to an end through default.

It is easy to see, then, that it was not the payment of reparations that broke down the German economy. The fact is that Germany set out to evade her obligations and to get reparations payments cut down and cancelled as soon as could be done. To this end she was willing to take inflationary steps that would inevitably lead to the breakdown of her own economy. She was willing to ruin all her middle-class citizens. After the French occupied the Ruhr early in 1923 to compel the Germans to live up to their engagements, Germany did not hesitate to bring on an inflation that ruthlessly destroyed the old mark and wiped the Government's domestic debt slate clean. When years afterwards I was talking to Dr. Schacht on another matter I alluded to this action, and he spoke as if what he had done was easy as rolling off a log.

As we review the figures of German payments after World War I — and mind you! in that war not a foot of German soil was occupied, not an industrial plant destroyed, the physical means of Germany's production left almost untouched — I wish it were possible to get, by way of comparison, a trustworthy estimate of what Germany extracted from the conquered and overrun countries of Europe during World War II. Unfortunately no such estimate has come to my attention; and probably none can ever be made because of the complexity of the problem involved in arriving at figures on a comparable basis for all the countries concerned. But it is clear that, if we could reach any trustworthy estimate, the figure would be so large as to make the amount collected by the Allies from Germany after World War I seem insignificant.

This is indicated by the magnitude of the estimates hitherto published. For example, Professor Atwood H. Townsend has put the figure for "thefts of plant and machinery, objets d'art, furniture, cattle, etc.," at 25 billion pounds. Other unofficial estimates published in

The New York Times, and referring to Europe alone, put the loss in "loot, official and private," at $100 billion or about the same as Townsend's estimate. Research experts of American University at Washington, D. C., have estimated that about $80.6 billion was looted.

These estimates were all made before the war ended in Europe. They apparently do not include costs of occupation imposed upon the European countries by Germany and collected under duress. Nor do they include contributions forced upon the occupied countries of Europe under clearing agreements with respect to trade between them and Germany. Finally, they apparently do not include Russian losses, estimated by the Soviet Government at a figure corresponding at 1941 prices roughly to $57 billion, although this amount probably represents material damage and losses as a whole rather than German loot and occupation costs alone.

While we must, therefore, concede that the available estimates are not altogether reliable (and owing to the very nature of the problem could not be precise), the figures are so stupendous as to indicate again how mild were the ideas of the Allies as to the amount they would exact from Germany following their victory in World War I. In the light of all this it is not difficult to understand how, after the comparatively light burden that Germany assumed as a consequence of her World War I defeat, the Prussian military chiefs fell in readily with the idea that for her to wage a new World War (II) was a very fair business risk. They never dreamed that their own industries and cities would be destroyed by the Allies from the air.

At Paris twenty-eight years ago we were unduly disturbed over the question of "transfer," that is to say, how Germany was to find the francs and the sterling to pay her bill for reparations. If she paid it in the form of goods and services, that meant that Germany's manufacture and export trade would be stimulated to the point where it became a serious competitive menace to the respective economies of the Allies. That was a problem that Britain and France never solved — how to help build up Germany so that she would become just prosperous enough to pay reparations, and yet not successful enough to become a trade menace.

The new technique is much simpler. Just follow the example that Germany herself first set in the countries that she conquered in World War II, that is, go in and take away everything of value. That has been the course followed by Russia in her occupation of Eastern Germany after World War II. When Germany overran Western Russia in 1941 and 1942 she looted and carried off everything useful that she did not destroy. Russia has been following Germany's example on a grand scale. She has taken away as much as she could in the way of machinery and goods, much of it probably useless to her.

Now Russia is insisting upon siphoning off reparations from Germany's current production. That scheme would mean that Germany's sustenance would be removed before she had a chance to get back on her feet and earn a living for herself. It would mean that America chiefly, Great Britain in part, would have to continue to feed the Germans — in effect paying to Russia the reparations due from Germany, an intolerable situation.

Some individuals believe that we could buy the good will and friendliness of the Soviets by paying out of our own pockets the amount of reparations due to Russia from Germany. I take no stock in such naive belief. Meanwhile, at any rate, we and the British are continuing to feed the Germans at a cost of hundreds of millions of dollars every year.

The reparations question at Versailles twenty-eight years ago should, of course, be studied in the light of the conditions then existing after World War I, of the economic and social disorder that then prevailed on the continent of Europe. It should be studied with realization, as I have just suggested, of the much greater difficulties facing the world today as a result of the more devastating struggle of World War II.

15

GERMAN FOOD CRISIS, 1919

Our work on reparations was interrupted in late February by the so-called food crisis in Germany. I have been reminded of this recently in reading current dispatches from Germany about the food shortages and the semi-riots staged by the Germans in demanding the bettering of their food conditions in the American Zone. In a Berlin news dispatch to *The New York Times* dated May 17, 1947, it was stated that the current economic crisis in Germany could be attributed largely to the "soft" policy pursued by the British and Americans in their occupation zones during the last eighteen months. This indicates again how 1919 history is repeating itself today. The following extracts from my personal diary at Paris bear striking comparison:

> February 24, 1919 — Big conflicting reports as to conditions in Germany, but net is that blockade is still severe, food scarce, and ominously for first time in generations Germans have stopped working. It all points to the urging of speedy peace.

> February 27, 1919 — Spent evening listening to oral report from a Dr. Davis just returned from Germany. He says: "Nobody working—general apathy and numbness—pensions pauperizing people. Men saying they are bankrupt

morally and every other way — revelations about faked
import and agricultural statistics."

It was only a day or two after those news dispatches
in 1919 that Mr. Lloyd George stormed into a meeting
of the Economic Council and threw a bombshell among
us all. He declared that according to reports from his
General Plumer, in charge of British occupation forces
in Germany, the Germans were starving. "I tell you,"
said Mr. Lloyd George, "my people, the British people,
will not stand this. We cannot let people starve before
our eyes, no matter what their behavior has been."

We promptly pointed out to the British Prime Minister that, in an agreement made with the Germans subsequent to the Armistice, they had obligated themselves
to turn over the entire German merchant fleet as an act
precedent to the delivery of food to them. They had
failed to turn over a single ship. They had refused to
pay out any of their gold for food.

The British Prime Minister declared that all such
facts might well be true, but that again his people would
throw him out if we failed to take some relief steps. So
it was then and there decided that a considerable delegation of us should as promptly as possible meet the Germans at Spa in Belgium and see what could be done.

Thus on March 3rd a lot of us took the train for the
Spa mission. Arriving there late on the following afternoon we arranged to meet the German delegation at
6 P.M. I wrote out longhand a sort of picture of that
meeting. Perhaps I can do no better, by way of comment on the German mind, than to insert herewith my
picture as I wrote it at the time:

GERMAN FOOD CRISIS, 1919

Spa

March 4, 1919, 6 P.M.

A long, bare table—great high windows—the twilight grey of a March day, trees spreading bare and brown in the courtyard outside. Along one side of the table 20 Germans — not all German-looking. Von Braun in the middle — Prussian military mustaches — at his right Melchior (partner of Warburg banking firm), close cropped hair — melancholy. Back of the first row 45 aides, secretaries, and interpreters. On our side another 20. British Admiral Hope presiding — U. S. at right, G. B. at left, then Italy, France on our right. 20 behind us.

At 6 P.M. sharp we file in with Admiral Hope at head—Germans all standing. The slightest possible bow by Hope — more of one from Von B. Hope clears his throat and reads — at the end of every sentence, a German officer translates into German, a Frenchman into French. Whispered comments by Germans as the reading proceeds.

Dusk grows deeper and dim electric candles begin to glow from the side walls. The monotonous reading goes on, followed by the German translation. Suddenly the lights drop out and we are left in almost darkness. They flash up again and the reading goes on. But the light keeps dim and the gloom thickens. Someone brings in candles stuck in Rhine wine bottles and the German delegates carefully shove them out to exactly the middle of the table.

The British shipping man begins to read his conditions and more animated whispering follows by the German delegates. An old bearded German, kindly looking, leans back, fixes his eyes on the ceiling and follows the translation with strained attention. Most of the others look sulky or indifferent. All the conditions set forth are clear and unbending.

Then Von B begins in German with his eyes fixed on the table, and as we have no interpreter, the German interpreter puts it into English for us. He says the turning over of the German fleet should depend upon contract signed to furnish food *till next harvest*.

Again the lights go out and we are left for a little in almost total darkness, with Von B's voice coming slowly out of the gloom. He finishes just as the lights spring up again. He turns to Dr. Melchior and asks him to discuss finance.

Keynes answers and explains that we had not considered
370M tons of food as lasting to harvest. His statement is clear
and clean cut. Von B replies and again says fixing of all food
up to harvest must be arranged before fleet will be turned over.
He suggests break-up into Sub-Committees on Finance, Food
and Shipping, and meet tomorrow morning.

Admiral Hope replies and says of course we expect to send
more food but unless they hand over ships there are none to
carry food. Besides which they signed agreement to turn over
ships. Again Von B replies and says they have a public opinion
in Germany to deal with about turning over the ships. Keynes
replies and summarizes. Says that a month has been wasted
because Germany has not lived up to agreement.

Von B again takes up the argument and goes over the same
ground again, talking of the danger politically in Germany of
further delays. Keynes answers again and says we appreciate
all these points. We will do all we can if you keep your agreement. Von B moves adjournment. Hope says we cannot work
in Sub-Committees till the ships are turned over. Hopes that is
not last word of Germans. Von B says he can say no more till
he confers with Government.

March 5, 1919, 4 P.M.

A brighter scene than last night. Outside the sun shining
brightly from a clear sky. Von B begins his reply — regrets
that communications with Weimar so bad as to have caused delay. Goes over old ground. This time we have our own interpreter — so Von B hands it out in German and it goes first into
English and then into French. As Von B goes on we begin to
bet whether the Boches will climb down or not. It is a dramatic
moment when Von B comes to the point of declaring their
position. They throw down the gauntlet. They offer to deliver
fleet pro rata to food delivered. He took 50 minutes to make his
statement, with English and French translations. Adjourn for a
few minutes to look over German Government proposal more
carefully.

½ hour discussion by all of us. Then became active in helping to prepare brief contra statement. The Germans file in again
at 5:35 and Keynes makes our statement. Gloom deepens on
faces of the Boches as their interpreter goes on and outside the

dusk begins to gather. Von B says the statement contains no new factor. It becomes plain to me that we cannot get together.

A discussion goes back and forth on questions of construction of the agreements following the Armistice. I am not sure but that there is some honest difference of appearance here between construction of English and German versions. It is clear that they are camouflaging about the delivery of the fleet, with the hope of getting from us an agreement about food up to harvest; knowing that if we give such agreement, they will be free from pressure for food in any negotiations for the Treaty of Peace.

The Germans end up by practically acknowledging that agreement turning over of fleet must precede delivery of food, but they adhere to stand — must have assurances as to future food.

We break up with tentative plan to meet 10 A.M. March 6. Dinner with the American General in command, visited the headquarters that the Kaiser had occupied and also General Hindenburg's cave. Bed at 10:30. At 11 note from Von B, conciliatory but n. g. We sent short note in response at 3:30 A.M. Met and started for Paris.

Returning to Paris, Albert Strauss of the American delegation and I made our report as to the outcome of the Spa meeting. My diary says:

> March 7 — Reported to Col. House at 9:30 results of Spa trip. Our junior delegation met at Secy. Lansing's office at 10:30 and talked over plans. Plain that arrangement must be made to work out whole thing or crisis would come. I suggested resolution for Supreme War Council to pass, giving Supreme Economic Council authority. Went over to Sup. Economic at 12. Lord Robert Cecil presided. Serious and earnest determination to put thing through and overcome French opposition.

At Mr. Lloyd George's request I met him and Philip Kerr to give him a word-of-mouth report. The yellowed memorandum on this talk that I find among my papers says:

> Memorandum of conversation held on Friday noon, March 7th, 1919, there being present Mr. Lloyd George, his Secretary Philip Kerr, N. H. Davis, and T. W. Lamont.
>
> First, Lloyd George asked TWL for a brief report of the meeting at Spa, and the result thereof, which of course he had received also from other directions.
>
> Lloyd George agreed with the expression made, that the Germans were not entirely unreasonable in their attitude, and he felt with us that the situation could be straightened out only by agreement of French to act with us and make with us binding assurances to the Germans of sufficient food to supply them during the first few months. He described in detail his conversation with Clemenceau of this morning on this particular point, and said that while he was not absolutely certain, he felt pretty sure that Clemenceau would go along and approve the plan for solving the difficulty and for meeting the Germans half way. He said that Clemenceau felt so strongly against the Germans that he would be sure to turn down any proposition that came from the Germans; that, therefore, we must see to it that whoever presented the proposition of compromise at the Supreme War Council, presented it as the proposition of our side, and not from that of the Germans.

Mr. Lloyd George's remarks made it clear that we must meet the Germans again and fix up a *modus operandi* on the question of food and ships. This is of some interest to me in the light of present-day events. Germany had clearly broken her agreement as to the exchange of foods and ships. Nevertheless her people were very hungry, or at least they said they were, and so we had to make concessions, be "soft," as the present-day *New York Times* dispatch puts it, and meet their needs. Thus my diary of March 8, 1919, mentions "a most interesting and thrilling meeting of the Supreme

War Council." The next day at a meeting of the Economic section at Colonel Houses's office it was decided that Hoover (Food), Robinson (Shipping) and I should go to Brussels and put the thing through — that is, arrangements for feeding the Germans.

My diary goes on, from Brussels:

March 13 — Met Boches Hotel Astoria at 2. Very interested in Boche attitude. Seemed in a way not to realize they were licked. Insisted we must give them unsecured credit for food and must let them export gold to neutrals. Otherwise "their credit would be injured." Perhaps they thought to get us to realize that if we did not we should be ruining them for reparations. But they shied at having a toe cut off when next week the whole leg must come off.

Admiral Wemyss (British head of our delegation) put up our shipping proposition. At 3 we split into Sub-Committees, and Finance, Keynes at head, worked until 7:30.

March 14 — The final plenary session furnished a suspense. After the whole thing had presumably been fixed up Von Braun said that their instructions did not permit them to sign unless we promised to meet them in 8 days to discuss matter of unsecured credit and unless we promised to undo the black list. Admiral W. looked flabbergasted, didn't know the way out. I wrote on the paper table cover in front of me for Admiral Wemyss' eye (a Boche twisting his neck off to read it upside down). "In the Finance Commission our people gave the Germans general assurances that we should take up the blockade question actively. Why don't you give a formal declaration to same effect and see if it doesn't go?" I saw the Admiral buck up. As soon as Von B finished he cleared his throat, looked with a cold stare at Von B, read out my statement and added in solemn tones — "In the presence of this delegation, I declare that I will give my personal attention to this blockade matter." Von B said "In view of the Admiral's declaration, we will sign." And sign they did. To

me it was illustrative of belief that when it comes to peace
they will struggle hard but *sign at end*.

Thus, through large Allied concessions, the food
crisis in Germany in 1919 — we never knew how really
serious it was — was surmounted.

Herbert Hoover was of course of invaluable aid
throughout the Conference. He had completed his
gigantic war task of feeding the Belgians which gave
him world-wide fame. He had brought succor to the
Poles, and had done all that Bolshevik Russia would
permit him to do — except under impossible conditions
— for the Russian people.

Hoover was in Europe before the Conference got
under way, and with his extraordinary experience was
naturally the chief organizer and moving spirit of the
Supreme Economic Council. Aside from such bad food
conditions as may have existed in parts of Germany,
there were scattered about Middle Europe various
plague spots where hunger and desolation demanded the
attention of the Allies. Thus Mr. Hoover was leaned on
pretty heavily and always had his hands full. He was,
however, never hesitant to tackle a new job if it needed
to be done, and his attitude was never negative. If reconstruction were possible in any given situation, then
Hoover moved forward to take it up. It was in that
spirit that he was the leader of our Conference at Brussels, to try to reach agreement with the Germans. Knowing more about food and its prudent handling than all
the rest of our small delegation put together, Hoover
naturally was the one to make a final size-up of German
conditions and of the good faith of their appeals.

It was in May of 1947 that Mr. Hoover spoke a warning to our authorities in charge of the American Zone in Germany, and pointed out that in some way or other the German farmers must be made to disgorge surplus stocks of grain for their needy fellow citizens. I am not at all sure that, when issuing his recent warning, Mr. Hoover's mind did not revert to the situation that prevailed in Germany in March, 1919, and that he and the rest of us attempted to meet in the Brussels Conference at that time.

16

INTERVIEW WITH KERENSKY

Paris in 1919 was all agog from the chatter of Russian refugees who had fled their native land after the murder of the Czar and his family early in the preceding year. Each individual of the lot had a new solution to offer on how to get Russia back into the community of nations. Most of their plans contemplated armed intervention, this time on a greater scale. But Lloyd George and Woodrow Wilson and Georges Clemenceau had had enough of that, and so these half frantic émigrés were largely shunted off on us junior members of the Allied delegation, or found no audience at all.

Finally Alexander Kerensky appeared on the scene, Kerensky who had been the middle-of-the-road premier and for six months of 1917 had tried his best to hold Russia in the war. Yet he was far too much to the left to suit the run-of-the-mill émigrés, the counts and countesses with the memories of past generations at the Czars' court still before them. Even for him the Big Four had no time.

I was asked to find out what Kerensky's formula was, for he had sent word that he had one that would work.

I welcomed the suggestion that two of us should interview him, and my good friend Felix Frankfurter (for
years past now an eminent member of the United States
Supreme Court) agreed to join in. He and I invited
Kerensky to dine with us in a private room at one of
the first-class Paris restaurants. We talked from seven
o'clock that evening until 3:30 A.M.

Kerensky was spirited and interesting. But he could
not avoid making a series of speeches to Felix and me.
He would leap to his feet and stride about the room in
his earnestness and sincerity. As the night wore on,
with half-closed eyes I would lean back and gaze at the
faded pink satin panelling of the old French chamber
where we were dining, until the walls became dreamily
transformed into tiers upon tiers of misty auditors,
gazing down upon the former minister of a great state,
"Th' applause of listening senators to command." Then
I would catch myself up, and Frankfurter and I would
again begin our futile questioning. But the former
Prime Minister could not get down to earth. Certain
of the qualities that had marked him in 1917 as lacking
in incisive leadership showed clearly through that
gloomy evening.

Again and again I would stop Mr. Kerensky and say:
"But, Mr. Minister, look here. Tomorrow morning at
eleven o'clock I am to meet the Big Four and am pledged
to give them an oral report of what your formula is.
What is this surefire plan that you have sent word you
have? What do you propose that we do? Give us a
time-table. Tell us, A, B, C and so on, the successive
steps you want the Allies to take. We must have some-

thing definite, Mr. Frankfurter and I, or we shall be powerless. The Allies regard the Russian situation as of the gravest importance. You are the only one in Paris who has held high government position in Russia. For the sake of Russia, for the peace of the world, tell us what you think we should do."

That was in effect the theme that Frankfurter and I, who were in perfect accord, kept pounding on all night long. But it was useless. Next morning I had to tell the Big Four that we had got nowhere with Kerensky, that he had no workable plan to propose for handling the Soviets.

At my invitation Mr. Kerensky, who has been living in this country for some years, came to luncheon with me only the other day (December, 1947), and again impressed me as an individual of great honesty, imagination and fervor. He had recently written a letter to the *New York Times*, reiterating the same belief that he held in 1919, namely, that the Soviet despots represented only a few hundred thousand Russians, and that their dictatorship could not continue indefinitely. He was certain that, despite the secret police system, there must eventually be an overturn in Russia, and that the present rulers would be thrown out.

Indeed I hope with all my heart that Mr. Kerensky may be right. Yet I look back over the almost twenty-nine years since our meeting in Paris when Mr. Kerensky was as firm in his belief as he is today. Whenever I meet Mr. Justice Frankfurter we recall that fruitless evening, our disappointment, our questioning as to whether we could have handled things to a better end. When we were asked to be the ones to talk with Kerensky, we felt that it might prove a great, a fateful opportunity. It proved hopeless.

17

PERSONALITIES AT THE CONFERENCE

On President Wilson's return to Paris in March, 1919, after a six weeks trip to the United States, he had a bad case of influenza and out of courtesy to him the conferences on the drafting of the treaty were cut down from the original Council of Ten and became meetings of the Big Four, held usually in the afternoon at the house occupied by Mr. Wilson. It was chiefly at this house in the Place des Etats Unis that we so-called experts were able to get a close view of the Big Four: President Wilson, Mr. Lloyd George, M. Clemenceau, and Premier Orlando.

Woodrow Wilson at the Peace Conference was the same Scotch mixture of wonderful idealism and stubbornness that he had proved himself to be in positions of importance that he had occupied before he became President. He had a delightful personality, a ready wit, was one of the most agreeable men that I have ever been fortunate enough to work with. The soul of honor, he was not given to playing politics, although he did have an unfortunate distrust for every Republican in public life and hardly a good word for any of them. He had shown this prejudice in his choice of members of the

American Commission to Negotiate Peace when he failed to choose ex-Senator Root or some other active Republican to join the Commission and thus gain political support for ratification of the Treaty.

President Wilson clung to his idealism and imbued the entire delegation with it. In fact, we almost reached the point where we felt that the American delegation was the only one that was working for an unselfish, just, and tolerable peace, and that all the other delegations were engaged in grinding their own axes. Throughout the Peace Conference in 1919, I never witnessed an occasion when I saw Mr. Wilson moved by an unworthy conception or motive, unless you can call his yielding principle to compromise that, where certainly compromise was essential.

The President's mistakes in judgment were, however, by no means infrequent. I have already alluded to his lamentable blunders on matters like leaving the Chinese province of Shantung, even temporarily, in the hands of the Japanese (Japan would never have left the Conference); in his handling of the matter of Fiume which drove the Italian delegation from the Conference; in his judgment, too, as I have always thought, on the Reparations question — in that instance his failure to insist upon the naming of a definite sum in the Treaty itself for the Germans to pay.

Yet no one could work with Mr. Wilson without enormous respect for him and complete confidence in the integrity of his intentions. Harold Nicolson in his *Peace-Making 1919* speaks of the high opinion of President Wilson held by Arthur J. Balfour, Britain's Foreign

Minister. He quotes Mr. Balfour as saying of the American President that he was astonished "that he is as good round a table as he was on paper. His attitude at the meetings of the Big Four was firm, modest, restrained, eloquent, well informed and convincing."

Mr. Lloyd George was a live human being and his personality was attractive. Day by day he was a charming man to work with. He was not continually trying to bamboozle Mr. Wilson or anybody else, as Maynard Keynes would have had us think. In fact I recorded in my diary at the time of the conference Mr. Lloyd George's belief that "the only real League of Nations that we can depend upon for the long future is the action together of America and Great Britain." And I noted that he expressed himself as most gratified with the manner in which the British and American delegates were working together on almost every question that came up.

Yet Lloyd George was a politician first, last, and all of the time, and a Welshman on top of that. Some of his own people adored him, others detested him. The British Prime Minister had nothing like the idealism that marked President Wilson. He was bound to keep a close eye on his constituency back home. What he wanted was always to do just the right thing, provided it did not impair his party's political position unduly.

In outright negotiation Lloyd George frequently had the better of the President, because he had the trading habit of starting far ahead of his goal, then of being able to give the impression of heavy concessions and still arrive at some point near what he was aiming for.

M. Clemenceau's personality was, if anything, more striking than those of the President and of Mr. Lloyd George. He sat there in his armchair afternoon after afternoon, his hands invariably clad in gray gloves, his eyes sometimes half closed, losing not a single word that was spoken in the room, whatever the language might be. He had equal facility in English and in French, years before having been in America as a teacher. But of course he preferred his native tongue, and insisted upon its being used when anything of importance was on the carpet.

President Wilson back in 1919 seemed to think that if you had a perfect plan that existed on paper, and the object was a worthy one, then it could without too much difficulty be made to work. M. Clemenceau was manifestly skeptical of such idealism. Day after day Clemenceau sat there, seemingly immobile, yet suddenly flashing into life and, with the patient and cynical logic that marks every brilliant Frenchman, making comment that almost completely devastated some rather high-flown utterance of Mr. Lloyd George's or Mr. Wilson's.

Orlando, the Italian Premier and the fourth of the Big Four, had a first-class mind and high integrity, but had difficulty in carrying out his own judgments. Orlando was a man of great charm and excellent education. For years before he entered politics he had been a professor of law in one of the Italian universities. Although today he is well along in his eighties, he is still the grand old man of Italy.

In addition to the Big Four, there were other leading individuals at the Peace Conference about whom I would like to set down a few paragraphs. These men have all played a part in the destiny of their respective countries, and, because the world has grown so small, of the world as it is today. It would be difficult for me to give any idea of what my five-months' close association with these individuals has meant to me in all the after years of my life. And I must emphasize once more the earnestness, the unselfish purpose, and the outstanding intellectual integrity of these men. I have been proud to call them all my friends.

General Jan Christiaan Smuts of South Africa was of course outstanding, as he would be in any group, in any age. Having, in his several brilliant campaigns, driven the Germans out of South Africa, he was summoned to take an important part in the deliberations at Paris. His counsel was excellent, and he had such capacity that his services were utilized for matters beyond the Conference itself. Everyone remembers the story of how, when the Welsh coal miners struck in 1919, threatening a stoppage of industry and disaster to the British community, Lloyd George asked Smuts to go down to Wales from London and see what he could do. Smuts arrived at one of the chief coal-mining centers, and an immense crowd gathered in the open air to hear what he had to say. He spoke nothing of the strike. He said nothing of the war. He talked to the Welshmen of their singing and of their choruses for which they were famed the world over. He asked if they would not sing for him their inspiriting hymn "Land of Our Fathers." And so the wonderful chorus of thousands of voices swelled forth, echoing from the surrounding hills. When the Welshmen had finished General Smuts thanked them and told them briefly that it was for them to see to it that Wales and all Britain were kept strong and safe, as the "land of our fathers," safe from enemy or alien hands. Then he went back to London. Next morning Mr. Lloyd George said to him: "How in the world did you do it?" "Do what?" asked General Smuts. "The strikers went back to work last night," was the Prime Minister's response.

The only blot on General Smuts's escutcheon with the American delegation was that it regarded General Smuts as all wrong when he advocated the inclusion of pensions in the Reparations bill against Germany. By no processes of reckoning could any of our counsel figure that pensions were other than war costs that, as a claim against Germany, had been ruled out at the very start. But Smuts wrote a persuasive memorandum on the subject, and President Wilson swallowed it whole. When John Foster Dulles (who had prepared a convincing brief on the matter) and the rest of us juniors waited upon him and urged him not to include pensions, he would not listen to us.

"Mr. President," I said, "there is no logic in such a policy."

"Logic? Logic?" he said. "I don't give a damn for logic! I am going to include pensions." One could well join in his sympathies, yet disagree with his logic.

In the years between the two World Wars General (now Marshal) Smuts's repute continued to grow throughout the world. My friendship with him, formed amid those crowded days at Paris in 1919, has been a great pride and satisfaction for the rest of my life.

Italy's Foreign Minister, who at Paris was next in command to Orlando, was Baron Sonnino, half Italian and half Scotch, very brilliant, but on the whole hardly commanding the confidence of any of the delegations, including his own. He was an astute, aggressive, and frequently successful negotiator.

Greece's Prime Minister, Eleutherios Venizelos, was an outstanding individual. I became pretty well acquainted with him and was impressed with the character of his statesmanship. He had had a hard row to hoe at home, with King Constantine hanging around his neck, and Constantine was an impossible individual. Venizelos made a moving, and on the whole successful, appeal in behalf of Greece on the territorial settlements. Later in Athens, when King Constantine lost his throne, the situation of the local parties became more and more confused, and eventually Venizelos lost his working majority in the Greek Parliament. He was an elderly man by that time and his retirement would in any event have come before long. With his withdrawal from politics, and death a year later, the government of Greece fell into less and less capable hands, and so continued during the ensuing years.

Eduard Benes, later to become head of the Czechoslovak State, was a new star in the firmament, almost unnoted until the middle of the Peace Conference. He proved himself at Paris to be a statesman of great acumen and skill. A man of broad education, he had studied at the university at Prague, at the Sorbonne, in Berlin, and in London. As a professor of history at the University of Prague, he had come to have complete knowledge of

Europe's past, with a thoroughly adequate idea of what her future ought properly to be.

At the time of the break-up of the Austro-Hungarian Empire, Bohemia, which was the center of Czechoslovakian enterprise and culture, became with its leading city Prague the basis for the new Czechoslovakian Republic, established by Thomas G. Masaryk, known generally as the father of his country. At the time of the Peace Conference, however, he was advanced in years, and his son Jan Masaryk was too young to assume too much responsibility.

To my thinking, Dr. Benes stood out in sagacity and effectiveness from all the other delegates of the states composing the old Austro-Hungarian Empire. When, after we had finished work on the Treaty with Germany, we were asked to turn our attention to Germany's war allies, and decided that certain of the new states of the old Austro-Hungarian Empire ought to pay something in the way of reparations, a great wail of protest arose from those states, with the exception of Czechoslovakia. Benes said that he thought that the attitude of the Allies was a reasonable one, provided the burden was not made unduly great, for his country was impoverished. This attitude established him at once high in the esteem of all the Allied leaders.

I was so impressed with Benes's broad-mindedness that I begged Mr. Lloyd George, who had only met him formally, to send for him. Lloyd George was immensely interested in him, took him up and worked with him earnestly for several years to help solve the problems of Central Europe. Although later they did not always see eye to eye, the fact remains that Benes, of all the individuals active in the old Austro-Hungarian Empire, has been the only outstanding one to endure and remain as the leader of his nation, largely I think because of his genius for political composition.

In the years following World War II, Dr. Benes, like the other leaders of Czechoslovakia, realized that his country was in effect in Russia's power. He stated this fact emphatically on more than one occasion, and the result was that for a time the Soviets were inclined to let Czechoslovakia pursue its own policy, which always contemplated active working contacts with the world of Western Europe and with America. The Soviet Government has recently taken steps (I am writing in July, 1947) preventing Czechoslovakia from attending the Paris Conference, called to formulate a pan-European plan to implement Secretary Marshall's idea. For centuries the products of Bohemia have been sought throughout the Western World. I cannot believe that with one stroke of ruthlessness the Soviet Government is going to be able to destroy that trade.

During the years following World War I, Dr. Benes worked steadily for European and world security. But the European world ignored or rejected his far-sighted plans. In 1936, when Germany started to march into the Rhineland, Benes begged England and France to stop Hitler for all time by holding to their obligations under the Locarno Treaty. They failed to do it and that was the beginning of the end. Many laudatory adjectives have been applied to Dr. Benes. He is a brave man, a statesman who takes seriously, not himself, but the world. I have been greatly honored by his continuing friendship.

Ignaz Paderewski, the new Prime Minister of Poland, was a delightful and rather pathetic figure at the Conference. He represented a country of ancient tradition and culture that had for centuries been the battleground of greater powers and that, within a century and a quarter, had been sliced up — three "Partitions of Poland" that had served to keep the country as a satellite but had never broken the spirit of her gallant, though rather impractical people. Paderewski had great personal appeal for all of us. I recall the dinner, in the course of the Conference, that Mr. Herbert Hoover gave to him in order to have some American men of affairs who chanced to be in Paris meet him and hear from him direct the great value of Poland's material resources. We had a pleasant dinner and at the end, at Mr. Hoover's request, Paderewski launched into an interesting recital of some of Poland's available resources, like coal, timber, forests, and so on. For an individual who was first of all an artist, he did very well at the job.

After he had finished I remarked, "That is very interesting, Mr. President, but what about your relations with other powers? Will everything be tranquil? How are you going to get along in the future, for example, with Germany?" "Oh, Mr. Lamont," he replied, "we shall *always* be fighting Germany. We have never been at peace with Germany. We never shall be." That admission was rather a damper for the Americans who were listening to him. But at least it was frank.

In any category of outstanding figures, Lord Robert

Cecil of the British delegation should always be mentioned — the youngest son of the old Marquess of Salisbury who had been Prime Minister under Queen Victoria and who was one of Britain's outstanding statesmen of the Victorian era. Lord Robert was of the highest possible character, of outstanding integrity, and with a great sense of fairness. He was a man of deep religious convictions. He could also fight better than most of the British delegation for what were the true interests of his own country, and he never hesitated to take a firm and insistent stand on any matter of principle that affected Britain.

Lord Robert, who was afterwards created Viscount Cecil, was between the wars a factor in British politics. Although he is now advanced in years, his word always commands deeply respectful attention. Personally he was one of the most delightful individuals at Paris. Throughout all his advancing years, and certainly today, he has maintained the same charm and enjoyed the same confidence that complete integrity of character always commands.

The brilliant Lord Curzon was in and out of the Conference a good deal. He had made a notable viceroy of India in the early years of the century, chiefly however, I may say, in splendor and magnificence rather than in his capacity to work out many of the pressing Indian problems that over the years have come to such a head. He too became the author of the so-called Curzon Line that was laid down as a fair scheme for the eastern boundary of Poland and that we have heard much of since.

One day Mr. Lloyd George asked me to see Lord

Curzon on a question — I forget the exact nature of it — with which he thought I was particularly familiar and might gain Curzon's concurrence upon. So I waited on his lordship who, while observing all the rules of protocol, was high and mighty and let me go after a brief and unsatisfactory interview. I told Mr. Lloyd George of the disappointing results. Whereupon Mr. Lloyd George, with a whimsical smile, said musingly, "Well, you know how much store Curzon sets upon his ancient lineage and noble birth.

"Do you realize, Lamont, that if on that June day early in the eleventh century Robert, Duke of Normandy, had not been cantering through the forest, and if, just as he passed a lowly cottage there, the breeze at that moment had not lifted the skirt of the lovely daughter of the household who came tripping out to the gate, and of whom the Duke became straightaway enamoured, there might have been no such individual as William the Conqueror, and we shouldn't have George Curzon with us today!"

I could go on and add to the list, but now I will only mention Philip Kerr who was secretary in the larger sense to Prime Minister Lloyd George, and who afterwards as the Marquess of Lothian was a most successful British Ambassador to the United States, his tenure, just prior to the outbreak of World War II, coming to an end with his lamentable death at Washington.

Kerr and I became warm friends. He was a fascinating individual, with a gay and brilliant mind, great intensity of purpose and an almost romantic sense of public duty. Kerr had been one of that gallant band, Lord

Milner's "kindergarten" as it was affectionately called, which, fresh from university, went out to South Africa just after the Boer War almost half a century ago and did so much, with General Smuts's cooperation, to bring about peace and stable conditions. This group, which also included John Buchan (Lord Tweedsmuir), Robert Brand (now Lord Brand), Lionel Curtis, Geoffrey Dawson, late editor of the London *Times*, prepared the way for the country to become, as the Union of South Africa, one of the great members of the British Commonwealth.

At Paris Kerr spent most of his time trying to hold Mr. Lloyd George back a bit, and astonishingly enough frequently succeeded. Kerr was one of those who did not at all agree with President Wilson as to the workability of Article X of the League of Nations Covenant. More of that, however, I set forth in the following chapter. Here it is enough to say that Kerr fought a good fight to have the Covenant avoid that great weakness, namely, the ill-starred attempt to give political, coercive powers to the League of Nations. But Mr. Wilson would listen to no one on that particular phase.

Lloyd George had for his staff of experts rather a mixed grill, — some of them like Lord Robert Cecil and Maynard Keynes (until he went home in a huff) being outstanding. The minor civil servants from the Foreign Office and other departments, men like the brilliant Harold Nicolson, were competent and extremely helpful to him.

As to President Wilson's fellow plenipotentiaries, he failed almost completely to utilize their counsel and services. The one notable exception was of course Colonel

House. But it has to be said with considerable regret that after the President's return to Paris from America in early March, 1919, he rather cold-shouldered Colonel House who, as the weeks went by, became less and less in touch with him, less and less in his confidence. This change was of considerable consequence and, as most of us juniors thought, unfortunate.

Colonel House was the one man in America who from the early years of World War I, long before America became engaged in it, made not infrequent trips to Europe, established contacts there in both London and Paris, and then in Germany itself, where he talked with the Kaiser, the Chancellor, and other leaders. As one of the four American plenipotentiaries other than the President, House came to the Conference better equipped with knowledge, experience, and acquaintance with all the parties with whom we had to deal than anyone else. He was regarded most highly by them all and was trusted completely.

I will not attempt to go into the causes of his fall from grace, nor to sift all the gossip that went about the council chambers in Paris in that fateful spring of 1919; I will merely say that the charge that, in the President's absence in Washington during January and February, Colonel House had made certain commitments which clashed with the principles laid down by the President had no basis in fact.

As for the four other plenipotentiaries, the President turned his back on them. His own Secretary of State Robert Lansing, a man of good common sense and considerable experience, even though not a whirlwind in

action, was called at the outset to attend the meetings of
the Council of Ten. But when that Council was reduced
to the conclave of the Big Four, from that date on the
American Secretary of State was completely ignored.
One reason for this was that he was opposed to the attempt to crowd through the completion of the League
of Nations Covenant prior to the active discussions on
the Peace Treaty itself. This idea was such anathema
to the President that he had no further use for Mr.
Lansing. Mr. Lansing's own book on the Conference
makes that perfectly clear. The point is that whatever
usefulness he originally had was lost to the American
delegation and to the Conference.

As for General Tasker Bliss, undoubtedly it was important to have as one of the American plenipotentiaries
a first-class military man. That being the case, no one
better could have been picked out than Bliss, who was a
fine type, well educated in matters far afield from those
merely military. He took an intense interest in the proceedings and tried his best by furnishing memoranda on
this, that, and the other topic, to make himself useful.
He had sound ideas about the League of Nations, about
Reparations, and about many other matters. I always
found him a mine of intelligence and interesting ideas.
But for the American delegation in the Conference those
ideas were largely lost. As for Henry White, more than
once he sent for me, to explain with a grim smile that he
had little notion of what was going on, and would I
please be good enough to give him the news.

In failing so largely to utilize the minds and capacities
of his fellow peace plenipotentiaries and by attempting

to go it alone, President Wilson handicapped himself greatly, both in the extra physical exertion that he was obliged to make and in the loss of ideas from his own contemporaries that might have been of great relief and value to him. His failure to consult his aides more intimately was not, as alleged by some, due to his desire to gain complete credit for himself, but rather to a habit of non-consultation which must have dated back in his career for many years. It is no disloyalty to the memory of a truly great man like Woodrow Wilson — and assuredly he was a great man, as all history will bear witness — to point out such personal failings as these that I have touched upon, especially because they worked so seriously to his own disadvantage.

As to other personalities of the American delegation, there was a group of highly trained and intelligent experts in history, economics and other subjects, that had been gathered together by Colonel House, and that contributed enormously to the making of the Treaty, men like Professors Seymour, Coolidge, Bowman and Young. In addition, the group of which I was a member was made up of Norman H. Davis and myself, both representatives of the U. S. Treasury designated by the Secretary, Carter Glass, Bernard M. Baruch, Vance McCormick, and John Foster Dulles, the last of whom we considered as counsel to our group.

Davis and I, concerned chiefly with financial and economic matters, were preoccupied primarily with the reparations question, and, as I have indicated, we both acted severally and together upon the Sub-Committee of the Reparations Commission which was charged with the task of determining Germany's capacity to pay. Vance McCormick, whom I had known slightly years before when he was a student at Phillips Andover Academy and I at Phillips Exeter, and who had been chairman of Woodrow Wilson's campaign committee in 1916, was active on that phase of reparations that had to do with the categories of damages for which the Allies could properly lay claim.

Bernard Baruch was a roving ambassador. He had not come to the Conference charged with any one duty. But he made himself useful in almost every direction and showed the same capacity for handling problems and persons that he has always displayed. At times he was active like the rest of us on the reparations problem. He was a great favorite of the President and commanded his complete confidence. The intimate acquaintances that he cultivated among members of the British delegation from top to bottom were no doubt of great value to the President. We all worked together as an harmonious group, with all questions of precedence eliminated. Not long after the war Mr. Baruch wrote a volume on the Peace Conference called *The Making of the Reparation and Economic Sections of the Treaty*, which has always been utilized by students of the Conference.

All four of us placed great reliance upon John Foster Dulles, who was simply a younger edition of the mature statesman that he is today. By training he was an excellent lawyer, by mind and temperament he was a most valuable counsellor. We were free to turn to him on every occasion, as we did. It was Foster Dulles who prepared for us the perfect argument against inclusion of pensions in the bill for reparations against Germany, and it was that sound and valid brief that President Wilson set aside in favor of General Smuts's appealing argument for the inclusion of pensions. This junior group of which I speak had the good fortune each one to be a personal friend of the other. Two of them, Norman Davis and Vance McCormick, are no longer of this world, but the preoccupations and important work of Mr. Baruch and Mr. Dulles in post-World War II are a matter of public knowledge and praise.

18

TREATY SIGNING AT VERSAILLES

The great day of the signing had arrived — a beautiful Saturday morning, June 28. Norman Davis and I with our wives started before ten o'clock in one of those dirty-tan colored government cars for Versailles. The route was not too crowded, but French poilus stood at all the crossroads waving aside all but official traffic. As we started up the long and beautiful avenue leading to Versailles, the scene became gayer and more martial. On either side up to the Château the avenue was lined with French cavalry in steel blue helmets, the red and white pennants from their lances fluttering in the breeze. In the great court were more troops, and just where we alighted was gathered a group of French generals, Pétain, Mangin, Gouraud and others.

Up the great staircase we went, everything magnificent with hangings and rugs that the French had provided to make the spectacle an impressive and gorgeous one. The large hall (La Galerie des Glaces) was already more than half-filled. Not long after our arrival M. Clemenceau, looking old and more shriveled than ever, yet full of unquenchable life, came in and took his seat, followed soon after by President Wilson, Mr. Lloyd

George and all the other chiefs of state, sitting around a low dais. Sir William Orpen has made an excellent portrait study of the group.

Directly on the hour the low and constant chattering of the individuals, various functionaries and "experts" of the Conference like ourselves to the number of a thousand at least, is suddenly interrupted by a sharp military order. In the hush that follows M. Clemenceau, looking stonily forward, neither to right nor left, declares: "Faites entrer les Allemands."

In the silence we could hear the sepulchral sound outside of heavy footsteps gradually approaching. Preceded by four army officers of the principal Allies, Britain, France, Italy, and the United States, the two German representatives enter and proceed slowly down the aisle towards the dais. Their names mean nothing — Dr. Muller and Dr. Bell. They are utterly woebegone, deathly pale, more like ghosts than living men. They have been chosen as the scapegoats by the Weimar Republic which, as a republic, is already a joke, even if the Big Four and the rest of us do not know it. The two delegates are seated at the table with the mien of men about to sign their own death warrants.

"Messieurs," croaks M. Clemenceau in low but distinct tones, "la séance est ouverte."

Copies of the Treaty are placed before the German delegates, and with visible trembling they sign their names. Then the chiefs of state on the Allied side all sign theirs — there appear to be a score of them. It seems as if centuries were being lived in the brief few minutes before it is all over.

Suddenly the subdued chattering which has risen again during the ceremony is hushed and M. Clemenceau, still unmoved, croaks again: "La séance est levée." That is all.

The Germans are led out, like prisoners from a dock, and the crowd immediately prepares to depart, following the chiefs of state. I take my wife up to present her to M. Clemenceau, and just then the cannon outside, from far and wide, begin to boom, to signal that the defeated Germans have signed a Treaty of Peace!

"Ah, M. Lamont et Madame," says M. Clemenceau to us, "ceci est le son que j'ai attendu et que j'ai voulu entendre pendant quarante-huit ans!" And the tears are creeping down his weather-beaten cheeks.

Then we walk out to the terrace and look down the vistas of lovely trees to see all the fountains playing and sparkling in the sun for the first time since war began, with planes flying overhead and the paeans of victory still sounding from the cannon far and near.

"Oui," says Clemenceau, with tears still in his old eyes, "oui, c'est une belle journée!"

Thus the Peace was signed. But the peace that the chiefs of state and all of us aides had worked for and thought had come to pass was destined after all to fail.

IV

The League of Nations

19

WILSON'S FIGHT FOR THE LEAGUE

Had it not been for Woodrow Wilson's gallant fight—and death—for the League of Nations Covenant in 1919, the world today might never have had the United Nations Charter adopted at San Francisco in June, 1945. It took twenty-six long years for Mr. Wilson's noble conception to come into effect. Nations, like individuals, have short memories. Yet we Americans must never forget what Mr. Wilson's idealism contributed to the cause and organization of what we hope may be global peace.

Various versions have been given us of the battle that was waged over America's part in the League of Nations struggle in 1919-20. Some writers have contended that America's withdrawal was due wholly to President Wilson's obstinacy in refusing to accept reasonable reservations offered by the United States Senate. Others have declared that the whole trouble was due to Senator Henry Cabot Lodge of Massachusetts and a small coterie that surrounded him.

This chapter is written to show that neither of these extremist theories is tenable. From neither the Senate chamber nor from the White House did the Treaty and the League of Nations Covenant have a fair chance. In the end the Covenant lay dead at the hands of its friends and foes alike.

The first draft of the League Covenant was made public on February 14, 1919, and during the succeeding months in Paris I was able to witness at close range the workings of Mr. Wilson's mind in the Covenant debate, and was sometimes able to supply him with information that he seemed to lack about public opinion in America. I heard the comments (and criticisms as well) of some of the British and other delegates. The whole scene was like a play that developed week by week, each act of the play bringing us a bit nearer the final tragedy that befell in the ultimate Senate rejection of the Treaty and Covenant by the Democratic Senators themselves, acting upon the President's orders.

Many members of the public and even students of history seem to think to this day that the League Covenant was defeated by the votes of a Republican Senate. Of course this was not so. Upon President Wilson's instructions to his party Senators, forty-two Democrats, with only thirteen Republicans, voted on November 19, 1919, to defeat the Treaty with reservations. On March 19, 1920, twenty-three Democrats, under Mr. Wilson's instructions, voted to kill the Treaty with reservations, only twelve Republicans following suit.

And these reservations were simply against certain phraseology which was not at all serious, which Britain and other nations made clear they favored, and which was in effect embodied in the United Nations Charter at San Francisco in 1945. President Wilson's inflexible will, his unwillingness to stoop to conquer, his refusal to compromise, his determination to have precisely his own wording or no Covenant at all, had killed the League.

Thus the actual facts make it clear that neither the all-saint theory as to Mr. Wilson nor the all-devil theory as to Senator Lodge can hold water. As in the case of all great political struggles, victories or defeats, the result of the Covenant failure was due to no one single person or group. It was the product of many minds and motives working at cross-purposes. The resulting tragedy — and I insist upon calling it at least that although "catastrophe" might be the better word — was one that could, without great difficulty, and should have been prevented.

Few commentators on America's rejection of the League Covenant have made it clear enough that the one greatest stumbling block to ratification was Article X. It was the commitment in the first sentence of Article X that aroused such apprehension and criticism, President Wilson's wording being:

The Members of the League undertake to respect and to *preserve* as against external aggression the territorial integrity and existing political independence of all Members of the League. In case of any such aggression or in case of any threat or danger of such aggression the Council shall advise upon the means by which this obligation *shall be* fulfilled. (My italics)

It was of course the general and sweeping obligation ("undertake . . . to preserve") set forth in the first sentence of the Article that aroused antagonism from so many important quarters. It was the character of the commitment expressed in that first sentence of Article

183

X that led Senator Lodge, and Senator Knox as well, to urge so strongly that the adoption of the Article would contravene the American Constitution by depriving Congress of the power to declare, or to desist from declaring war.

Senator Root, if his services had been requisitioned at any time by President Wilson, would have been able to suggest workable modifications of Mr. Wilson's wording — a wording which seemed to pledge America to a moral commitment to defend for an indefinite number of years to come, the score of European national territorial boundaries set up under the Versailles Treaty.

I have never ceased to believe that had the President not rejected, in the most kindly but firmest manner possible, the several urgings that he invite ex-Senator Elihu Root to come to Paris as a counsellor to the American delegation, an entirely different result would have been achieved. Root's opinion and support would have carried immense weight with all the Republican members of the Senate, including Henry Cabot Lodge, who had a wholesome respect for Root as clearly the elder statesman of the Republican Party, if not of the whole country.

Prior to Mr. Wilson's departure for the Peace Conference he could readily have sent for the Republican leaders in the appropriate Senate and House committees to counsel with them, just as twenty-five years later President Roosevelt did, and to give them some of his ideas. Next, of course, he could have named as one or two of the five Commissioners to the Peace Conference high ranking members of the Republican hierarchy.

There again, although he was particularly urged to adopt this plan, he failed to take the preliminary steps to enlist the cooperation of his political opponents.

Thus at every stage of progress the contrast between his tactics and Mr. Roosevelt's becomes clearer. It was those errors of omission and commission, of which Mr. Wilson was guilty, that became proof positive to his Democratic successor of a quarter century later that, in the matter of any organization for world peace, his policy must be thoroughly cooperative with that of his political opponents.

After Wilson's first triumphal visit to England and the Continent he had returned to Washington in late February, 1919, for the closing session of the old Congress. He took with him the initial draft of the Covenant, and I think we all expected that he would take occasion to explain to our public, as well as to the leading members of the Congress itself, just what the Covenant was designed to accomplish and how it was composed to that end. Thus, all those of us, including Colonel House, who were anxious that no serious obstacles should hinder the League ratification, were distinctly disappointed that the President, in no one of his public utterances, clearly took occasion to explain the significant features of the Covenant. When weeks afterwards, and well after Mr. Wilson's return to Paris, Senate and press opposition to the League began to crystallize at home, it at once became apparent to all those who had studied the Covenant at all that the attacks upon it were due as much to ignorance as to any valid objection.

To be sure, the President on the way home from Paris

in February had by wireless invited the members of the Senate and House Foreign Relations Committees to join him for dinner and a talk at the White House. This meeting took place on February 27, 1919. Senator Borah with his usual pig-headedness on all foreign affairs refused to go to the White House, declaring that his opposition to the League was complete and his mind closed. Senators Lodge, Knox and Brandegee were less churlish and came to the White House dinner. But in all their subsequent private utterances that promptly became public they were ill-mannered and sweepingly critical, while Senator Brandegee had the effrontery to declare that the evening was like the Mad Hatter's Tea Party in *Alice in Wonderland*.

By all unprejudiced accounts of the meeting, the President had handled himself with great dignity. He had frankly stated that the Covenant did not attempt to spell out in detail what would happen in every possible contingency for years ahead. He made clear that the League was intended to be a living and growing instrumentality which, given the close association of good-willed nations upon its Council and Assembly, would be adaptable to fresh situations.

Yet at the close of Wilson's trip to America, Mr. Morgan cabled me as follows:

March 6/19. Politics is the most awful mess I have ever known it. Congress passed the bond bill fortunately, but declined to pass the railroad financing bill, Army and Navy appropriations bills, and various other essential measures. By this act they imperil the financial future of the Government for no purpose as as far as anyone can see except to snap at President. Latter has on the whole done badly since his return, because he has not been intelligent in his answers to criticisms on League of Nations plan, and he has not put it forward in anything like as favorable light as it deserves. Financial conditions are overshadowed by political ones.

When Mr. Morgan referred to the President's failure to give public exposition of the League of Nations plan he was undoubtedly alluding to Mr. Wilson's speech in Boston on his arrival from Paris, and again to his brief address at the Metropolitan Opera House in New York on March 5, 1919, on the night that he sailed on his return to Paris. On the first of these occasions, that at Boston, Mr. Wilson took the line that it would be premature to report on the proceedings of the Conference, but since America was the hope of the world, the results would be unthinkable if she did not justify that hope. He had shown his confidence in the ultimate victory of the Covenant by declaring: "I have no doubt of the verdict of America."

In his talk at the Opera House, on the eve of his sailing and before an attentive audience, President Wilson again confined himself to generalities and appeals to American idealism. He ignored his opportunity to expound simply and persuasively the plan of the League of Nations to an American public that was well disposed towards such a project, but really had had no explanation of the points set forth in the Covenant which Mr. Wilson had brought back with him. At the same time he injured his cause by flinging a quite unnecessary defiance at the Senate. All along ignorance on the part of the public, rather than innate opposition, was largely responsible for the lukewarmness of the American people.

America's failure to ratify the League of Nations Covenant in 1919 and 1920 was due to no lack of support and devotion by Mr. Wilson's immediate followers. That loyalty, however, did not make all those of us who were working around him at Paris blind to his errors of judgment. Woodrow Wilson's greatest weakness was in his estimate of human qualities, of the jealousies and fears and prejudices that beset mankind. Throughout all the long months at Paris in 1919, perhaps even to the very end, he seemed never to conceive the idea that, with the Covenant once a completed document, it would not be ratified without qualification by a thumping Senate majority. Perhaps among his advisors I was the one that entertained most doubt on this point.

My immediate business associates in New York and I had always been strong for the League, and had so expressed ourselves. President Wilson was aware of this fact, and more than once expressed satisfaction with it. Yet when repeatedly I relayed to him the messages that I received from home, indicating decided disaffection among leading Republican Senators, not to mention a severely critical editorial attitude on the part of certain influential newspapers, Mr. Wilson, as I could see, did not take the caution too seriously. He clung tenaciously to his conviction that upon his return to Washington carrying the completed Treaty and Covenant, serious opposition to their ratification would fade out.

During these 1919 spring months at Paris, my associates at home, most of them strong for Mr. Wilson's League, were uneasy about the growing opposition to it. I had previously on February 15 cabled to Mr. Dwight

W. Morrow asking him to give me a general idea of press comment in America, especially that of the old and staid *New York Evening Post,* of which I was the proprietor. Morrow replied that the *New York Times* and the *New York World* and the *Evening Post* were pro-League; that the *New York Sun* was distinctly against it; and that the *New York Tribune* (this was prior to the merger of the *Herald* and *Tribune*) was on the fence. The *Tribune* did not like the Covenant as drawn, stating that it "impairs the sovereignty of the United States and causes us to give up the Monroe Doctrine for a bogus league and rope of sand . . . the President is trying to usurp the power of the Senate."

In another message that Morrow sent me he alluded to the attitude of the so-called liberal press, which condemned the League Covenant as a miserable compromise, representing Wilson's abandonment of his ideals. Morrow spoke particularly of the criticism and complaint directed against the Covenant by the *New Republic.* *The Nation* took almost the same attitude. Both these journals, which in later years became bitterly critical of such part as was played by Lodge and other Republican Senators in the defeat of the Covenant, were at the time in effect in the Lodge camp, being clearly against the Treaty as it was presented by the President. There is always a question as to whether the perfectionists or the isolationists work the most mischief. How many old sayings have been written regarding the destructive attitude of these 100 per cent idealists! How many times have we implored them "not to let the best be the enemy of the good"!

I sent a further message to New York early in March asking a categorical question: "Do you still consider the situation in America as being dangerous to serious delay in final ratification of treaty that contains Covenant?" Without attempting a categorical reply, Dwight Morrow sized up matters when a few days later he cabled to me:

> I should sum the situation up substantially as follows: The country is very receptive to some kind of League of Nations. At the same time the opposition to certain features of the proposed Covenant is crystallizing and will be very strong. Bear in mind that most of the people in America — especially the women — are for a League of Nations because they are opposed to war. As Europe becomes more and more turbulent there will, in my opinion, be a growing reluctance to cast in our whole lot with Europe when it may seem to mean continued immediate participation in European boundary struggles.

His last sentence was manifestly an allusion to the vague commitment in Article X.

As a result of his own study of the Covenant, as well as the discussions in the press and among public men, Morrow again pointed out to me in a message on March 19th the inherent difficulties in Articles X and XVI of the Covenant, these being the ones that were most controversial, and the ones around which the implacable opposition in the Senate finally centered. Of course upon his return to Paris I gave President Wilson copies of my cable exchanges, and also sent copies to Colonel House who was greatly impressed with the continued gravity of the situation regarding a possible upset in Senate ratification. These messages from Dwight Morrow, later Ambassador to Mexico and then Senator from New Jersey to the time of his lamentably early death in 1931, always seemed to me sound, but President Wilson, who more than once emphasized to me his confidence in the objective nature of these comments, was disinclined to take advantage of them.

About this time in a further message Morrow said:

> More than one-third of the new Senate has signed a round-robin stating that they are opposed to the plan as now drawn. The danger is that men will get set so hard one way that they will feel they are fighting for a principle and will go down rather than yield. The main difficulty is, in my mind, that no one has authoritatively explained for the Peace Commission what the plan really means.

In this same message Morrow made the rather striking suggestion:

> It would be most helpful if someone acceptable to the President and in whom the Senate has confidence could be with him in some sort of capacity. It would be great help if someone like Senator Elihu Root, who is not opposed to the President, could be associated as counsel. Would there be any chance of having both Senator Elihu Root and Justice Brandeis sent for as joint counsel for the Commission?

Morrow's suggestion was of course a common-sense one. We were all aware, as the President himself must have been, of Senator Root's patriotic attitude. The additional idea of having Brandeis go over was a sound one. Brandeis was known as a great liberal and was one of President Wilson's first appointees to the United States Supreme Court. But it was not to be. Reviewing all these messages, the President still took the ground that any such designation of Root as counsellor in the then state of affairs would be "a sign of deplorable weakness."

Among the delegation members at Paris there was continuous talk to the effect that the President had determined to be his own counsellor on matters of the League. Thus, it was on March 11th that at a dinner to the French journalists I sat next to General Tasker H. Bliss who spoke freely to me of his relations and those of the three other Commissioners to President Wilson. He said in so many words that the President would allow no one of his associates on the Mission to have anything to do with the League of Nations, "would accept no suggestions from them and told them it was his affair and they were not to butt in."

Ray Stannard Baker, who was utterly devoted to President Wilson, says in one of his three volumes on Wilson at the Peace Conference: "Lloyd George apparently consulted Balfour and General Smuts more than Wilson consulted Lansing or House, or Bliss, to say nothing of White who was rarely consulted at all." There is no doubt that President Wilson considered the League of Nations project as his particular idea. And in that field he ignored the views of his fellow Commissioners.

Although I had nothing whatsoever to do with the drafting of the League Covenant, yet, being constantly thrown with members of the task force that was working on its composition such as General Smuts and Lord Robert Cecil of the British delegation, I was frequently listening to bits of their discussion about the framing of the Covenant. Philip Kerr frankly expressed his judgment that the language of Articles X and XVI should be permissive rather than mandatory. He said clearly that he did not wish his own country, Britain, to be virtually committed, if not to make war, at least to impose economic sanctions and embargoes at the drop of the hat on any country that, at some distant time, might be adjudged to be an aggressor. He expressed the belief that America might similarly shy away from such a seemingly mandatory commitment. More than once Kerr urged his chief to adopt his own attitude towards these decidedly bugaboo articles. But Mr. Lloyd George was the easy-going optimist. If America would stand for mandatory action — and he quoted the President as declaring she would — then Lloyd George guessed that Britain could afford to go along.

Even at the risk of taking myself too seriously, and despite all the President's most polite rebuffs, I continued the effort to get Mr. Wilson to open his mind on the question of reasonable amendments to the Covenant. Later in March I showed a memorandum to the President, embodying Senator Root's views in somewhat greater detail. Root fully appreciated the great difficulty which the Peace Commission was facing in trying to get accord on any programme. He thought there were many commendable features in the plan, notably the great step forward that it made in insuring common counsel on political disputes before war is entered upon. But he felt that the guarantee of political boundaries in Article X committed the various nations including the United States of America to intervention in many boundary disputes with which they were not concerned.

I ought perhaps to have known that any suggested modification of Article X, as advocated by Senator Root, would be anathema to the President. It was then or a little later that he had termed that Article "the heart of the Covenant."

Throughout those crowded weeks at Paris I continued to be so convinced of the beneficent purposes of the League Covenant, and so apprehensive that near-chaos would soon reign on the Continent unless an early peace were declared and ratified by the United States Senate, that I continued to work away against the American opposition. Enterprise throughout Europe had come to a standstill. That was naturally true of the enemy countries, but Allied and neutral countries likewise were in a state of suspended animation. Thus, although I feared that it would be of little use, I went out all the way in one direct message to an old acquaintance, Frank Munsey, publisher of the *New York Sun*. I quote some passages from my cable to him and his reply:

April 9th. Because I know that your criticism is always honest and patriotic I have been particularly concerned to feel that the attitude of the *Sun* has been really such as seriously to endanger the success of the Covenant. The views of many important governments have been so divergent that the only hope of getting an instrument that all will be bound by lies in taking advantage of the present situation to compel each one to sink some of its individual ideas in order that a common basis may be reached. To try to begin the world afresh with no provision against future war is unthinkable. I earnestly hope that the *Sun* will see its way clear to point out that recent amendments have gone far to meet the just criticisms made in America. If you show the way other influential Republican journals will follow.

From Mr. Munsey:

April 23rd. I am very glad to have your cablegram and fully understand your fine patriotic purpose. Holding strongly to the view however that this country should remain free and become a big stabilizing force among the nations of the world, I cannot favor any instrument that would hamper our free action or tie us up in a Covenant with discordant nations, many of them mere tribal nations. I fully realize America's responsibility, but I am convinced there is nothing that this country should be called upon to do as a member of a League of Nations that it would not cheerfully do free from covenanted compulsion. You may be assured that the position of the *Sun* has rested on no petty political or personal prejudice but rather on absolute conviction.

To all my efforts regarding the League, of which I have described only a part, the President had always made cordial response. In a letter to me dated at Paris June 7th, he said:

I deeply appreciate your letter of June fifth enclosing a copy of the message from your partner, Mr. Dwight Morrow. I know the disinterested spirit in which you are thinking about these matters which are of such critical and fundamental importance, and hope you will permit me to say that I have more and more admired the liberal and public-spirited stand you have taken in all our counsels. . . .

The key to the whole matter is the truth, and if we can only get the people at home to see the picture as we see it, I think the difficulties will melt away.

It seemed to me at the time and it appears now, after I have read almost everything on the subject of the tragic clash between President Wilson and Senator Lodge, that it was due primarily not to the verbal omissions or commissions of the League Covenant which Lodge was talking about, but to the fundamental cleavage in ideas between the two men as to the handling of the main peace settlement. Lodge's faith in a democratic Germany was as tenuous as President Wilson's was firm.

Lodge was for the France that Clemenceau and Marshal Foch believed in; Mr. Wilson felt that France was chauvinistic and was too fearful of the new Germany that he envisaged. Both Lodge and Root were strong for the proposed Tripartite Treaty of defense for France against Germany. In Mr. Wilson's make-up idealism was overwhelmingly powerful, realism secondary. Just the opposite can be said of Lodge, who added cynicism to his realism. Mr. Wilson was uncompromising and obstinate, except with those who he believed were in fundamental agreement with him. Lodge was suspicious, bitter, ungenerous. His private memorandum, given to Henry White to show to Lloyd George and Clemenceau—the memorandum that undertook to belittle the President's political strength and cast grave doubt upon his idea of the League of Nations—was certainly lacking in scruple as well as in propriety.

Late in March Mr. Wilson let it be known that his mind had at last become more open on the subject of reasonable amendments to the Covenant. In that month ex-President Taft and President Lowell of Harvard, leaders of the old League to Enforce Peace, and anxious for the fate of the Covenant, sent to President Wilson a strong message urging that an amendment be inserted "more specifically safeguarding the Monroe Doctrine." They predicted that if this were done the Treaty would be "promptly ratified."

It was about this time also that Mr. Root, in response to an urgent cable from Colonel House, submitted six amendments. Colonel House made a great effort to have the Root amendments adopted as submitted, but by the time they got through the drafting committee's fine-tooth comb process they had been weakened to such an extent that they were no longer acceptable to the open-minded Root himself. Various other changes, however, suggested by President Taft, the League to Enforce Peace, and by Justice Hughes were embodied in the Covenant, but not in form satisfactory to all their authors. The President was at last clearly making some attempt to meet the situation, but would not put through the particular changes that would meet the views expressed at home.

By June Wilson's attitude again stiffened in respect to reservations. It was brought to a head on June 25th when, a few days before the Treaty signing, there had come through by cable to the President copy of a letter that Senator Root had written to Senator Lodge, calling for more specific interpretations of several clauses of the Covenant. In this very temperate letter of his to Lodge, Senator Root, consistent with his long-time advocacy of an association of nations, emphasized the constructive features of the League, and then went on to point out certain of them that should be eliminated or interpreted. The principal one of these was Article X which he felt should be cut out entirely. His conviction on this point was in line with the very criticisms of Article X that he had made in the messages transmitted to me from Mr. Morrow and Mr. Morgan, and that many weeks before I had urgently brought to the attention of the President at Paris. Senator Root's letter constituted to such an extent a guide post for the Republican Senators that it may be worth while to quote here some few parts of it:

There is in the Covenant a great deal of very high value which the world ought not to lose. The arrangement to make conferences of the powers automatic when there is danger of war; provisions for joint action, as, of course, by representatives of the nations concerned in matters affecting common interests; the agreement for delay in case of serious disputes, with opportunity to bring the public opinion of the world to bear on the disputants, and to induce cool and deliberate judgment; the recognition of racial and popular rights to the freedom of local self-governments; and the plan, indispensable in some form, for setting up governments in the vast regions deprived by the war of the autocratic rule which had maintained order — all these ought not to be lost, if that can possibly be avoided.

[But] nothing has been done to limit the vast and incalculable obligation which Article X of the Covenant undertakes to impose upon each member of the League to preserve against external aggression the territorial integrity and political independence of all members of the League all over the world. . . . *It stands upon its own footing as an independent alliance for the preservation of the status quo.* (My italics.)

If we agree to this Article, it is extremely probable that we shall be unable to keep our agreement. Making war nowadays depends upon the genuine sympathy of the people of the country at the time when the war has to be carried on. No general indefinite agreement made years before will make them disposed to fight. And we shall be in about the worst possible position of having made an agreement and not keeping it. Our people ought not to be forced into such a position, and we ought not to make any agreement that is liable to force them into such a position.

These were weighty and carefully considered views from a great American statesman who of all his countrymen was undoubtedly the one most experienced in world affairs. In this letter to Lodge from which I have quoted, Root goes on to show how staunch a supporter he would have been of the President's advocacy of a Tripartite Treaty with Britain for France's security. He wrote:

If it is necessary for the security of Western Europe that we should agree to go to the support, say, of France if attacked, let us agree to do that particular thing plainly, so that every man and woman in the country will understand the honorable obligation we are assuming. I am in favor of that. But let us not wrap up such a purpose in a vague universal obligation, under the impression that it really does not mean anything likely to happen.

Mr. Wilson, reacting sharply to the Root letter, cabled his secretary, Joseph Tumulty, at Washington:

My clear conviction is that the adoption of the Treaty by the Senate with reservations will put the United States as clearly out of the concert of nations as a rejection. We ought either to go in or stay out. To stay out would be fatal to the influence and even to the commercial prospects of the United States, and to go in would give her a leading place in the affairs of the world. Reservations would either mean nothing or postpone the conclusion of peace so far as America is concerned until every other principal nation concerned in the Treaty had found out by negotiation what the reservations practically meant and whether they could associate themselves with the United States on the terms of the reservations or not.

This message quite ignored the fact that Lord Robert Cecil, Britain's chief reliance for the Covenant drafting, was against Article X; that that was the stand taken by Philip Kerr (later Lord Lothian), Lloyd George's right-hand man; that General Smuts in his important draft Covenant had never suggested any article like No. X; that Canada's Prime Minister, Robert Borden, had been, and continued to be, bitterly against it. There was still that feeling on Mr. Wilson's part, which most of the delegation shared, that at the end opposition to the League would fade away, and that therefore its fate was not a matter of immediate concern at Paris.

20

LEAGUE OF NATIONS REJECTION

On June 28, 1919, the Treaty and League Covenant were signed at last, and most of us who were in the President's entourage started with him that same evening, to board the *George Washington* at Brest the next morning for the brief voyage home.

To me the President's return trip on the *George Washington* seems in retrospect to have been the only peaceful and happy time that he had had since the Armistice eight months before. He had during most of the period following the Armistice been battered about from pillar to post. Rushing over to Europe in early December of 1918, he had been swept through Britain and the Allied countries of the Continent, hailed as a conquering hero, his hours upset by the clamoring crowds of admiring people; speaking frequently in the open air in the great cities and under strain; enduring vagaries of climate, food, and sleeping conditions. Then came the excitement of the opening of the Conference, the awkwardness of getting it under way and, more important to him than anything else, the initial drafting of the League Covenant that to him was the backbone of the peace and of all that might come thereafter.

The President, at last free from the daily struggles at Paris, boarded the *George Washington* in an almost holiday mood. He had fought the good fight, had kept the faith and was now on his way home with the completed Treaty and Covenant, believing that his own country would fully support him. If he had any inward misgivings over the fact that had become so obvious — namely, the growing opposition at home to some of the terms of the League Covenant — certainly any such qualms in his own mind were so slight as not to affect his buoyancy and good spirits. In fact, he was comforted with a twofold reflection. First, he was satisfied that the Allied leaders had made sincere efforts to arrive at the just peace that, prior to the Conference, he had felt America alone stood for. Further, he believed, as I have said, that the peace that he was bearing home would appeal to the American people and that they would in effect say to him, "Well done, thou good and faithful servant!"

Thus after a day out of port, heading towards the west, the President began not only to rest and relax but to show signs of buoyancy and humor that had been absent from him for months. He paced the deck cheerily and chatted freely with any members of the delegation that happened to fall in alongside of him. And after a day or two he began the genial practice, about early teatime every afternoon, of ensconcing himself with Mrs. Wilson on the after-deck in the shelter of some of the topside structure, and of sitting there for an hour or two, gradually gathering around him the group that had worked so devotedly with him at Paris.

To none of us did he talk "business." His conversation

was in lighter vein, and before long we and those of us that had wives along looked forward keenly to this daily gathering. While we all joined in the chat, nevertheless, we naturally encouraged Mr. Wilson to do the talking. He was never didactic, always amusing, and frequently had us rocking with laughter over his essays in the field of limericks. It has always comforted me to know that President Wilson, after all his strenuous efforts at Paris, was at least able to have this brief space of happiness and recreation before having to face the dismaying realities of bitter opposition at home, of an exhausting "no-compromise" struggle, and finally of defeat and of death itself — death of the body, but not of the idea for which he had gallantly battled and which was destined in a later generation to develop into the United Nations organization of today.

My diary recalls some of the interesting discussions that we had with the President. One particularly I quote verbatim, because it gave such clear evidence that the President had changed his opinion radically as to Mr. Lloyd George and M. Clemenceau, and now thought of them as sincere statesmen, doing their best, not to serve their own countries' interests alone but to establish peace in the world:

July 5, 1919. President summoned us at 3 P.M. and read us his message to Congress in presenting the Treaty. It was skillfully done — a report in the large of his stewardship at Paris; of how the Treaty was worked out. He started as a basis with the work of our Army and what it stood for, paying it a fine tribute. "Our soldiers," he said, "were terrible in battle — gentle out of it." All Europe looked to us, he said. It became our business "to quiet the fears and encourage the hopes, etc." Then he went on to show how the Treaty had to be built upon the League of Nations.

At this point the President alluded to a tribute which he paid in his message to his colleagues (Lloyd George, Clemenceau and Orlando) for their unfailing sincerity and endeavor to do the right thing. My diary then runs:

W. W. said to be sure that was going pretty strong, but that he was actually convinced that on the whole the three others had made sincere efforts, in the face of many secret handicaps which they had. For instance, he said, when he first came over he had thought that they adopted the 14 points for the sake of policy and to end the War. But as he became acquainted with his colleagues he became convinced that they thoroughly believed themselves in the 14 points.

The President read us a series of titles for speeches on the Covenant that he intended to make if forced to fight for the Covenant. One title struck me particularly: "I don't want to wait and enter the League in company with Germany: I want to enter now."

Regarding the League and the growing opposition to it at Washington, I had had my say and there was nothing more to be done. Certainly so far as League fears were concerned, I was a minority of one in the Presidential party. In one of my previous letters to the President at Paris I had mentioned to him that not all my colleagues saw eye to eye with me on the question of the League prospects. And on the only occasion that we discussed the subject on the *George Washington*, one of them said to me in his always kindly manner: "Tom, we all appreciate your fears for the League. But you have been dead wrong right along about it. I have told the President that when he sets his foot on American soil with the Treaty and the League Covenant in his hand, the American people will get down and kiss his boots."

Indeed, when the President landed, from the uproarious welcome that he received, it almost seemed as if my colleague might be right after all. It was a great, spontaneous American greeting, and as Woodrow Wilson and the others drove up Broadway in open cars he was received with all the acclaim that America always bestows upon her great heroes. The crowds of welcoming New Yorkers felt that for him the long, hard day was ended. They wanted him to know their appreciation and their gratitude.

There was nothing within the gift of the American people and of the world that Woodrow Wilson did not deserve. There was nothing, I believe, that the American people and the American Senate itself would not have given to him, if (1) in that latter body there had been clear understanding, and (2) if only the President had from the very start handled the Senators more wisely. He had a proud and wilful Senate to deal with, and the only hope of salvation for the Covenant was, without discarding the substance, to make it reasonably palatable and above all, to make it understood. This is the course that Mr. Wilson turned his back upon; this is the course that illustrates so vividly the lesson that his successor, Franklin Roosevelt, learned and skillfully applied twenty-six years later.

No, the President still had that firm belief in the power and will of the people. He would appeal to them over the heads of all their elected representatives. They would respond and compel the Senate to ratify the Covenant. Hence, although he was tired to death and sorely in need of recreation, he planned an early autumn series of country-wide speeches. Neglecting himself, for others he had the utmost consideration. A few weeks after his return to Washington he wrote me from the White House a more than kind letter urging me to get some rest. But he added a characteristic and to me rather discouraging note about the Covenant:

> I hope now that all forces will be concentrated upon promoting the policy of keeping all reservations or interpretations out of the formal act of ratification, and embodying those that can reasonably be accepted in a separate document.

It was of course against the urgent advice of his physician, Admiral Cary Grayson, that the President, though his powers were waning, embarked on his long and arduous railroad trip to make a direct appeal to the country for his version of the League Covenant, as against the interpretations that the Senate was determined to attach to it. His speeches were still shot through with the fire of his idealism, that idealism for America that he constantly preached. I recall one ominous prophecy that he made. He declared, warning his Middle Western audience only too prophetically of what would happen if America failed to join the League: "There will come some time in the vengeful Providence of God another struggle in which not a few hundred thousand fine men of America will die but as many millions as are necessary to accomplish the final freedom of the peoples of the world."

The President was enthusiastically received and his addresses called forth warm applause. Yet it was support solely in behalf of the principle that America should take its proper place in this great plan for world cooperation. Never did Mr. Wilson's public detect any overweening virtue in the President's particular wording of various articles of the Covenant. Never was that public aroused enough to bring pressure on the Senate to adopt verbatim Mr. Wilson's Covenant, as against one with interpretations or reservations attached. In so far, then, as concerned the President's plan to fire the public to overrule the Senate on the question of phraseology, his trip was a complete failure. In so far as it constituted a strong temporary offset to the growing lethargy of the American people in the matter of foreign affairs, the trip was a great success.

The journey drew to its tragic end at Wichita in Kansas on September 26, 1919. The President returned to the White House a broken man. There ensued at the White House those long months of a sort of blackout when the President's condition was grave, when his physician would allow no one but his devoted wife and his immediate family to see him.

It was during this critical period, critical for Mr. Wilson, for his country, and for the world, that the most strenuous efforts were made to try to get some word to him that would lead him to open his mind on the question of the so-called "reservations," to leave the matter to the discretion of the Democratic Senators, acting under Senator Gilbert Hitchcock of Nebraska, their leader and wholly loyal to Woodrow Wilson. Mr. Wilson declined to talk with Colonel House who then begged me to go to Washington, thinking that, because at Paris I had been the one to beseech the President to consider the growing opposition, I might have some influence with him. But to interview Mr. Wilson even briefly just then was quite out of the question.

By all odds the most important effort to resolve the situation was made by the British Government. It sent over as Ambassador at Washington Britain's most distinguished statesman in the diplomatic field, Lord Grey, who in 1914, as Minister of Foreign Affairs, had been the one to lead in the declaration of war against a Germany that deemed sacred treaties to be merely scraps of paper. Lord Grey came over primarily for the purpose of seeing the President and urging him to accept *permissive*, instead of the textual *mandatory*, phrasings for the plaguey Articles X and XVI.

But President Wilson saw Lord Grey only on one or more formal occasions. Grey for long months at Washington sat and twirled his thumbs, in the vain hope of having a word with the President, of explaining to him that Britain considered America under no moral obligation whatsoever to adhere to any particular form of wording in the Articles in question; that if only the main principles and purposes of the Covenant could be agreed on, Britain was quite content to accept reservations and amendments and would herself promptly ratify such.

But it was not to be. On November 19, 1919, the Treaty with the Lodge reservations was upon the President's orders defeated by the Democrats themselves. The country was so shocked by this action that public opinion forced the Senate to get at the matter once more and to try to work out a plan of reconciliation.

Lord Grey, having failed in his mission, went back home. But he still refused to give up the ship. As late as February 1, 1920, when the Covenant was still being debated in the Senate and awaiting a second and final vote, Lord Grey took the unprecedented course of writing an open letter to the London *Times*, which was duly reprinted in the *New York Times* and given adequate publicity here. At London, and at Paris as well, there had been disappointment and dismay over the President-Senate deadlock, and Grey made this last appeal, in effect directly to Mr. Wilson and to the American public, for ratification of the Treaty and Covenant, even with reservations attached.

It is worth while reproducing a paragraph or two of Lord Grey's letter which incidentally went to show how much the mind of this statesman and that of Senator Root had moved along similar lines.

I do not deny that some of them are material qualifications of the League of Nations as drawn up at Paris or that they must be disappointing to those who are with that Covenant as it stands and are even proud of it, but those who have the longest experience of political affairs and especially of treaties know best how often it happens that difficulties which seem most formidable in anticipation and on paper never arise in practice.

I think this is likely to be particularly true in the working of the League of Nations. The difficulties and dangers which the Americans foresee in it will probably never arise or be felt by them when they are once in the League. And in the same way the weakening and injury to the League which some of its best friends apprehend from the American reservations would not be felt in practice.

If the outcome of the long controversy in the Senate is to offer cooperation in the League of Nations, it would be the greatest mistake to refuse that cooperation because conditions are attached to it, and when that cooperation is accepted let it not be accepted in a spirit of pessimism.

Lord Grey in his letter, which was reported to have given great offense to the President, was in effect doing little more than to emphasize Britain's traditional policy over the generations. Throughout the one hundred years from Waterloo in 1815 to 1914, when Britain with her mighty fleet maintained the Pax Britannica of the world, she made it her policy to make every effort to compose any particular international crisis that arose, but she avoided the practice of declaring *in advance* the precise nature of the intervention or mode of composition that she might undertake.

The fact that the French as well as the British press unanimously supported Grey's views as expressed in his letter was significant. In the light of that support from the Continent, as well as from Britain, the President's old argument that, if America attached reservations to the Covenant, that action would surely be followed by additional ones from all the Allied nations, lost all validity. What those suffering nations needed was to be assured of America's continued cooperation and presence in the post-war councils. The extent to which she might hedge about her cooperation with weasel-worded phraseology was of minor concern to them.

Yet even with this virtual statement from Britain that she preferred radical change in, or the elimination of, Article X, even with France's ready adherence to the same attitude, President Wilson clung obstinately to his determination to have his country enter into an indefinite commitment to maintain existing boundaries all over the world. Ray Stannard Baker has pointed out that the secret of the President's final determination to defeat the Treaty altogether, rather than have the Covenant fettered with reservations, lay in that ominous phrase in his letter to Senator Hitchcock: "These evil men intend to destroy the League."

That meant the end of everything. The fight was over. Wilson's final instructions from the sick room to Senator Hitchcock were again to vote down the Treaty with the reservations. And so on March 19, 1920, after the Senate had turned itself into a bear garden of frivolous debate, the Treaty itself and the League Covenant, with its principles of world cooperation and machinery for collective security still approved by possibly eighty out of the ninety-six Senators, were irretrievably lost.

It is indeed worth noting that some years later, shortly before his death, Senator Hitchcock, a high-minded and conscientious legislator, said to the distinguished President of Columbia University, the late Nicholas Murray Butler, who repeated the conversation to me, that the one thing he could not forgive himself in all his life was his acquiescence in the dictum from the sick President that the Treaty should be defeated.

I am well aware that many of President Wilson's friends always say, "Oh, no. Whatever compromise the Democratic Senators might have reached with Senator Lodge, he would have gone back on and brought out something more drastic to defeat the Treaty." This is mere conjecture. Senator Lodge, narrow-minded as he was and intolerant in his particular method of handling the League situation, nevertheless was Chairman of the

Committee on Foreign Relations in the United States Senate, and from that position had for years, together with President Taft, President Lowell of Harvard, and others, strongly advocated the principles of a collective organization for the preservation of peace. The record shows that Lodge twice voted for *ratification of the Treaty* with the Senate reservations attached. That is more than can be said of the Democratic Senators who, under orders from the White House, twice voted against ratification.

Among the consequences of the Senate refusal to ratify the main Treaty and Covenant were the failure of the Tripartite Treaty for the protection of France signed in Paris by Mr. Wilson, Mr. Lloyd George, and M. Clemenceau; our refusal to take a seat upon the Reparations Commission except "for observation," and our declining to take any responsibility in the mandate system of the League. An immense loss, too, for ourselves and for the world was the failure, after repeated efforts, to get the United States to adhere to the World Court, the importance of which most leading American jurists could not rate too highly.

With what melancholy can one imagine the thoughts that must have throbbed unceasingly through Woodrow Wilson's mind during all those weary months in the sick room! Vast issues, perhaps even the fate of the world, were hanging in the balance, were being settled beyond his power to control — unless he were willing through the acceptance of certain reservations, to compromise, as he thought, his own principles. For that noble and indomitable spirit that had to witness the great aspirations of his life blasted, the situation had the elements of a King Lear-like tragedy. With, as he believed, the menace of German militarism removed, the world held out to Mr. Wilson, under the constant cooperation among the nations as planned under the League, hopes of a millennium, of a new golden age of peace and prosperity. Surely, according to Woodrow Wilson's belief, one must have faith in a progressive reality, one must know that man can make superman, and that superman in turn can make supreme man. Yet the President as to his own reflections, his hopes, his fears, his resolves, was in the depths of a black gulf of solitude. He refused counsel. For salvation he relied solely upon his own unshakeable and unshaken will.

Sir James Arthur Salter in his recently published and most readable volume *Personality in Politics* speaks of a visit which Lord Cecil, one of the main architects of the League, paid to Mr. Wilson, ill and broken in his retirement in Washington. His mind was still clear as a bell. In their conversation, as retailed by Lord Cecil, Mr. Wilson broke in again and again to say: "We shall still win; no compromise." As Lord Cecil was starting to go, Mr. Wilson stopped him with a final injunction: "Remember," said the President, "no compromise."

In fact when Mr. Wilson had made up that inflexible mind of his, he was not content to feel that one might not compromise with sin: he seemed to feel that compromise in itself was a sin. Yet he was a student of history. He must have known well enough that some of the greatest triumphs of statesmanship that have been made over the centuries have been the result of compromise.

Even we men of affairs, being neither statesmen nor even politicians, have learned the necessity of compromise — of bargaining.

In the face of all mischance and of such errors of judgment as Woodrow Wilson committed, surely public opinion for all time will acclaim him as a leader of destiny. The world moves forward, not altogether blindly, but largely through individual action. An Horatius at the Bridge may change the outcome of an epoch or even the destiny of an empire. Woodrow Wilson was perhaps the stone cast into the stream that went to alter the course of a mighty river. The errors and frailties of human judgment we can forget. The mighty goal that Woodrow Wilson visualized for mankind and that he had to leave to others to reach we can never forget.

I was to see Mr. Wilson again only once. That was at the White House on a bright, sunny day in December, 1919. I had been requested by the Department of State and the British and French Foreign Offices to head a small commission to visit China and Japan, in the hope of straightening out some serious differences that had arisen between the three Western nations on the one hand and Japan on the other as to the scope and operations of the Consortium for the Assistance of China.

Mr. Wilson was at the White House in a wheel chair that was being rolled out into the big bay window through which the sun was streaming brightly. He greeted me most kindly and spoke for a moment whimsically of his own disabilities. He talked interestingly about my coming mission. I pointed out to him that in China itself the situation was anything but easy to deal with, by reason of the fact that at that period China was divided into two great factions: the North with its so-called Republican Government and the President of China established at Peking; the South with general head-quarters at Shanghai under Dr. Sun Yat Sen, the hinter-land being crowded with war lords of various strength and ill purpose. Mr. Wilson said to me half seriously, "Well, I think you must try to devise some formula that will help to bring the North and South together." And then he added, alluding to his birth and early youth, "You know, Lamont, traditionally I am always for the South." And he gave a little chuckle.

At the time of my visit the President seemed to me to have attained an astonishing degree of philosophy. He made no allusion to the bitter enmities which had so largely ruined a great world scheme. He had an unshake-able conviction that some day, somehow, the ideal of an organization for permanent peace would be fulfilled; that the setback which we had suffered was only one of those depressions that mankind must take in its stride as it climbs to the summit. At that time neither he nor any of us envisaged a Germany bent upon another effort for world domination. He took comfort in the belief that the natural idealism of the American people would in due course make itself manifest, and that the high hopes to which he himself had clung so desperately would be attained.

21

THE AFTERMATH

Behind all the bitter battle that was waged back and forth over the League of Nations, was the failure of the American people to understand that the United States of America held a new position in the world. America, as a whole, having certainly not been shaken by the war to its very foundations, had in no measurable degree seen the dangers of isolation, nor been convinced of the error of such a policy.

When once the country had turned its back upon the League, it grew more and more cynical as to any value in close international cooperation. In fact before many years a great body of belief had grown up to the effect that we had been drawn into the war, not by Germany forcing us to keep our own skins whole (which history manifestly showed to have been the case), but by a wily, perfidious and desperate Albion, plus American munitions makers and bankers who were thought to be so simple as to believe that war was a profitable instead of a catastrophically losing business.

Further, the publicity for the League had never been handled adequately from Paris or from Washington. In those days propaganda had not reached the fine art that it has today, and there was neither a Theodore nor a Franklin Roosevelt to make the cause an appealing and an irresistible one. The press, too, lacked sufficient guidance, in sharp contrast to the superb way in which the drafting of the United Nations Charter in 1945 was publicized.

In Ray Stannard Baker, President Wilson had a first-class man. But he was never given the staff, nor the information, nor the scope for public education on the topic of the League that it deserved. Instead of being furnished almost daily with a budget of journalistic material about the building up of the Covenant, what the newspapers got, to a very considerable extent, was rather a hint or more than a hint of the struggles and counter-struggles, the acrimonies, and the crises which various phases of the main Treaty discussion were meeting among the chiefs of state, and among the various delegations at Paris.

No, the American people were never thoroughly aroused to the dangers inherent in a world where tyrants and aggressors could still flourish. It never occurred to them in 1919 and 1920 that war and peace are indivisible — that it was possible to win the war and yet to lose the peace. It required a second World War, a Pearl Harbor and all that came after, to arouse America and to give her at last the conviction that international cooperation alone is the cornerstone for a peaceful world.

In June, 1920, I attended the Republican National Convention in Chicago. To me, there purely as a spectator—having never before been at any political convention—it was a dreary performance. The cause of international cooperation for which we felt that at Paris just a year before we had fought, bled and almost died was brushed off with a few innocuous utterances that meant nothing. Back to normalcy as fast as possible was the spirit of the gathering. Ballot after ballot followed between the two chief contestants, General Leonard Wood and Governor Lowden of Illinois—both of them of good repute, but not outstanding leaders to help reconstruct a world shattered and broken. When it was plain that the Convention was in a deadlock, there came "the small hours of the night in the smoke-filled room," and bright and early next morning word for everybody that it was to be Warren Gamaliel Harding of Ohio.

Our country had sent two million soldiers overseas, it had fought the good fight, it had helped "make the world safe for democracy." Withal, it had been turned from a debtor to a creditor nation on an immense scale. We had strength, vitality, infinite ingenuity and accomplishment in industry, vast wealth in agriculture, mining, and in every walk of life. But the change, holding out for us such immense opportunities for helping the world and ourselves at the same time, brought us no spirit of humility, no desire to complete the wonderful record of our men overseas.

Instead, we seemed to have acquired a sort of arrogance. The country felt that it could draw within itself and let the rest of the world alone — "They hired the money, didn't they?" Thus it was that America entered upon the new decade of the 1920s in full panoply of wealth and power, but possessing little ambition to realize her vast potentialities for strengthening the world in

stability and peace. That decade, with its exotic exuber-
ance of prosperity and its speculative excesses in almost
every phase of economic life, in farmlands and real estate
as well as in securities, was for America a decadent one.

A lifelong Republican, I cast my ballot for the first
time for the Democratic ticket in the Presidential election of 1920. My decision was of no importance except
to myself, but I will quote a few sentences from a letter
on the subject which I wrote to the *New York Evening
Post* when I was for a brief period its owner:

> In framing the policies of the *Evening Post*, you have had an
> absolutely free hand. Your decision to support Cox and Roose-
> velt was your own decision — not mine. But if, as a lifelong
> Republican, I had for a time certain misgivings as to your
> decision, I may now say that the developments of the cam-
> paign have resolved my doubts. I intend to vote for Cox and
> Roosevelt.
>
> My chief reason is, of course, that Cox is for the League of
> Nations and Harding is against it. The League is admittedly
> not perfect. But it is the most practicable instrument yet of-
> fered for the prevention of future wars. . . .
>
> Shall America, having taken her place in the war as champion
> of the weaker nations of the earth; shall America, having played
> her noble part in heroism and sacrifice, now take up the ignoble
> role of aloofness, of timidity, and of selfishness? Shall America,
> equipped in intellectual power and material resource to lead a
> world, now turn her back and, with clouded vision, reject that
> moral leadership which the lesser nations of the earth entreat
> her to assume?
>
> There is a call upon America to render high service to the
> world and to herself. To this call Harding answers No, let us
> turn back. Cox answers Yes, let us go forward. This is why I
> vote for Cox.

After Harding had been in the White House two or
three months, he sent for me to give him some informa-

tion on the intergovernmental debts. When I went in he was sitting rather gloomily at his flat-topped desk with a disarray of letters on one side of it. The President greeted me cordially, but said almost at once and with weariness in his voice, "Lamont, this job is just too much for me. Whatever shall I do with all that pile?" He gave a deep sigh as if he did not know just how to tackle the job, and then said, "Well, I suppose I might as well try to learn something about these debts."

As to the scandals that unhappily marked the Administration, nobody, I believe, could have been less a part of them than Harding himself; nobody would question his own good faith in public affairs. Harding was personally an honest man, without, however, much sense of discomfort in the society and friendship of men far less worthy than himself. He allowed himself to be surrounded by such men and they swamped him. He had in his Cabinet two or three outstanding individuals like Charles Evans Hughes and Herbert Hoover, but many of his cronies had far better claims as good poker-players than as statesmen. Harding himself had been brought up in a small-town environment from which, unlike some of our Presidents of modest origin, he never really emerged. Harding's chief interest for most of his life had been that little newspaper the *Marion Star*. That was his measure, and he never succeeded in enlarging it much. He was a pathetic figure, and was the last man in the world to lead 120 million people from the darkness and confusion of World War I out into the light.

To wind up the story of the League, I may add that seven months after President Harding came in, the Senate under Senator Lodge's leadership ratified a separate Treaty of Peace with Germany. What was the nature of the peace? It contained most of the harsh clauses of the Versailles Treaty; it emphasized once more some of the phrases that were most obnoxious to the Germans; it pushed in the pin pricks. We imposed the same restrictive clauses, economic and financial, as were in the Versailles document. We by-passed completely the ameliorating provisions that the League Covenant contained for the revision from time to time of such Treaty provisions as might ever become unworkable. And our refusal to allow any American representative to sit on the Reparations Commission was hardly less than a calamity. We turned our backs on all those constructive provisions for conference among the nations, and for meeting any international crises that might arise.

In other words, our separate Treaty with Germany embodied the most drastic and unworkable features of Versailles. It discarded the more liberal and workable ones. Senator Lodge had made no study of the working provisions of the Versailles Treaty. He utterly failed to realize that to make it practicable, and to make Germany work out her destiny under it, the Allies had all to act together or they were lost. If there were any validity at all to the criticism of the lip-smacking liberals here and in Britain that the Treaty was "unjust," the most unjust thing about it was that it was not enforced. As it turned out, America's defection was largely responsible for that failure.

Are there any lessons to be learned from examining some of the particular conditions that, in the hurly-burly of the twenty years between the World Wars, were largely brought about by America's having stuck to isolationism?

Certainly America's adhesion to the League, the sacred instrumentality for peace that she herself had proposed, was the world's only chance for thoroughgoing international cooperation and collective security for the preservation of peace. Our presence in the League Council could have made a strong vessel out of what proved to be a weak one. Our becoming familiar, day by day, through the contacts of our League representatives in Europe with the leading personalities over there, would have been revealing to a degree. With America in the League, would either Mussolini in 1935, or the Japanese in 1931, or Hitler in 1936, have dared launch so recklessly their several ventures in Ethiopia, Manchuria and the Rhineland?

We shall never know the depths of disappointment and dismay that our action brought to the friendly nations in association with which we had won the war. The two succeeding decades were marked by political deterioration in both Great Britain and France, especially the latter. We can by no means hold ourselves responsible for British and French sins of lethargy, lack of insight, and finally, fatal appeasement. But certainly our point-blank refusal to cooperate in the difficult peace served as a good swift kick to help the others on their declining way. Meanwhile, Germany was quietly rejoicing. The *summum bonum* that she longed for had been granted her: America had deserted her Allies. And Britain and France were beginning to fall apart, Britain's idea of a strongly reconstructed Germany (which at Paris we Americans shared) going directly counter to France's plea for safeguard against attack by a new and virile Germany.

There are those who argue that America's desertion of her Allies after World War I made little difference; that Germany, both her militarists and her people, had this inherited virus, this poison, itching within her and stimulating her to another attempt at conquest. Certainly the Herrenvolk had a megalomaniac lust for power, and the Germans, looking westward across the Atlantic between the wars, saw an America that gave every evidence of having written off any possibility of participation in a new conflict. They saw an America that had become the world's creditor nation, but whose people did not know how to behave as a creditor nation. They saw an America of immense but apparently unwieldly power, under the Harding administration, stick its head in the sand, and abjure the duties and responsibilities of world leadership that the country's own prowess and the fortunes of war had thrust upon it.

When you come to think of it the attitude of the American people was not after all surprising. For the century during which we had lived under the Monroe Doctrine, the British Navy had maintained the peace on the Seven Seas. There had been no cause for concern to us about foreign aggression. We had had such a comparatively peaceful world that we were inclined to feel that the War had been more of the nature of a hideous interlude than anything else, and that we need take no particular thought for the morrow. The minds of the people in Britain and here at home had been made sleepy by the continued glories of the long Victorian era. Mankind had been making wonderful advances in science, education, industry, and health. There had been nothing (except for those abnormal and unexpected war years of 1914-18) to shake earth's foundations and to endanger the onward march of civilization. Was it not natural for us all to expect that such progress should continue without serious let or hindrance?

To be sure, it was not so with President Wilson. The American public had, however, listened to his exhortations with gradually abating interest, and was only too inclined to turn its back on the whole business. Further, Woodrow Wilson's hopes that the nature of mankind had undergone an immensely favorable change were far too high for this erring world. "Human nature," said he, "has entered upon a new phase of its development." Even though his belief was unhappily ill-founded, yet at any rate Mr. Wilson was ready to fight and die for the change in the heart of man that he firmly believed was well under way.

Finally, between the two World Wars the American people made no earnest study of foreign affairs. They had enough to talk about that was of absorbing interest at home. They knew little enough of militaristic Germany. They, like the British, did not dream that a prosperous Germany would set out afresh to conquer her neighbors. In fact, if they thought of it at all, they were a bit hazy as to whether Germany, even with her initial violation and rape of Belgium, had started World War I. Our Americans of the 20th century were not the political philosophers that our forefathers, Franklin, Jefferson, Madison, Monroe, and the like, had been. We were too uninformed regarding the world at large, and too much absorbed in ourselves to drag ourselves from an easygoing past to the prospect of a possibly violent present. In foreign affairs we made no attempt to study the processes that make for good or evil.

We rather reverted to the generally distorted interpretation of Washington's Farewell Address and considered ourselves as a people apart. We knew ourselves to be endowed with immense natural resources, no boundaries that we had to defend, and a population extraordinarily industrious and possessing a genius for mass production in both industry and agriculture. We believed our security was insured by a geography that gave us two great oceans to provide defense from enemies abroad, and by the absence of neighbors of our own measure and strength.

The Treaty and the League having run upon the rocks, American public opinion that had had such a mild baptism in the vital ideas of international cooperation soon shook off the drops and the country went its own way. The reason was that among our people there was lacking that sense of personal responsibility, that knowledge that the business of preserving peace is not simply for our government officials, but for every one of us. So we fell by the wayside and failed in duty, first to ourselves, and next to the world.

V

China and Japan

22

INTERNATIONAL CHINESE
CONSORTIUM

I had hardly shaken the dust of the Paris Peace Conference from my shoes when I was compelled to start again upon my travels. This time they were to carry me much further afield — to Japan and China, with stops at Vancouver on the way out, and Honolulu on the way back. On this trip I was heading a small semi-official mission representing the International Consortium for the Assistance of China.

Away back in 1908, at the instance of their respective governments, British, French and German bankers had organized a group, later to be known as the Chinese Consortium, to handle loans for important constructive purposes that were required by the Chinese Government or by any of its provinces. In the last half of the nineteenth century there had quietly been imposed on China various "spheres of influence," largely utilized in a commercial way by several European states that had declared their several interests as paramount in these spheres, such as Britain in the Yangtze Valley, Germany in Shantung, Japan in South Manchuria, France in Yunnan, Russia on the Liaotung Peninsula. But after a time some of the European statesmen began, rightly enough, to fear that these several spheres in the Far East might clash and lead to larger conflict among the nations that sponsored them. There was the further point that a rather corrupt central Chinese Government would be completely "spoiled" if too many of the Western nations were competing for concessions, the value of which was at best exceedingly doubtful.

As for America, Secretary of State John Hay, in President McKinley's Cabinet, in 1899, had come out strongly for the "Open Door" in China, as being the only policy advantageous to China and fair to the trading nations of the Western World. Thus it was not unnatural that the later Taft Administration requested the British and French and German Governments to arrange for an invitation to be extended by the Consortium groups for the formation and inclusion of an American group.

This plan was carried out in 1909, and Henry P. Davison, representing an American Group, made up of J. P. Morgan & Co., Kuhn, Loeb & Co., The First National Bank and The National City Bank, joined in the deliberations of the Consortium at London. The first loan operation to China was one for the building of the Hukuang railway which was to connect Hankow with Chungking (to the west) and with Canton (to the south). The amount was £6,000,000, and the loan was issued, one-quarter each in Britain, France, America and Germany. Soon afterwards the Russian and Japanese Governments requested membership for their banking groups, so that the Consortium was enlarged to include six members.

228

For three years, as the European political scene grew more threatening, Consortium matters were quiescent. Then in 1913 Woodrow Wilson became President and William Jennings Bryan Secretary of State. Representatives of the Morgan firm at once went to Washington to ascertain whether the new Administration planned to follow the policy of its predecessor, which had invited bankers to establish a participating American group in the Consortium. We requested Secretary Bryan, in event of any change in policy, only to give us reasonable notice so that we might explain any such change in advance to the original groups abroad. Nothing, however, came from the State Department save silence. Suddenly after several weeks, with no prior notice, the White House issued a vigorous public statement, which was front page news, declaring that it had no use for the Taft policy towards China and that the American Group must be dissolved.

It was not because of prospective profits that the American Group was concerned by this sudden announcement, because Chinese Government business in itself had small attraction, but rather because the State Department had administered a wholly uncalled for affront to the British, French and German Foreign Offices, and because of the manifest concern shown in China by the withdrawal of America, which it had regarded as its staunchest friend.

However, *mutatis mutandis*. By 1916, when the Japanese had taken over Shantung Province the Wilson Administration executed a right-about-face. It addressed notes to Britain and France, calling for the reconstitution

229

of the Consortium on even broader lines than before and, wonder of wonders, pledged full diplomatic support to an enlarged American Group which it envisaged. We therefore increased the membership of the American Group to contain almost forty of the country's leading banking institutions, taking especial pains to include strong banks from the Pacific Coast. An organization meeting was set for Paris in the spring of 1919, at the time of the Peace Conference. I was asked to take the chair as a representative of the American Group. The organization of the new Consortium was duly completed along the lines proposed by the United States Government and favored by the British, French and Japanese Governments,— the German Government, in defeat, and the Russian Government, in revolution, being disregarded. The situation remained clouded, however, by reason of claims that the Japanese put forward regarding especial rights in Upper Manchuria and Inner Mongolia.

A lively exchange of diplomatic notes all through the summer and autumn of 1919 got nowhere. I was therefore asked by the American, British and French Groups, at the instance of their respective Governments, to visit Japan in the hope of reaching some composition with the Japanese.

23

BUSINESS AND PLEASURE IN JAPAN

When we were still sixty miles out at sea, we could see the snowclad peak of Fujiyama peeping out above the clouds. We landed at Yokohama at the end of February, 1920, my party including my old counselor, Jeremiah Smith, Jr., Martin Egan, an experienced hand in Far Eastern matters, my wife, and two intimate friends of ours, Jesse Lynch Williams and his wife. We were to be introduced to a Japan then under a so-called Liberal Government, but with the Emperor still a demi-god to all the people.

Japan was picturesque and beautiful in its outward aspects to one entertained, as I was, by individuals and families like the Mitsuis, the Mitsubishis, and the Iwasakis, — their houses and grounds wonderful and lovely to behold, their dinner entertainments entrancing. The noblewomen who were our hostesses were the living images, all of them, of the centuries-old Japanese prints that were scattered about the palaces. Japan's bankers who were my particular hosts were meticulously kind and hospitable, and able on every occasion of formal hospitality to produce from behind the scenes bevies of graceful, dancing geisha girls.

What of the military element, the caste that finally overrode all sense of liberalism in government and, twenty-one years later, led its country to Pearl Harbor and ultimate disaster? Yes, that must have been there, but much under cover. Every now and then one would come up against an intangible and subtle influence that seemed bent on a purpose that was sinister, and far from the lines on which outwardly all our discussions and negotiations were carried.

Almost at once we entered into active discussion with Inosuke Inouye, Governor of the Bank of Japan, an able, liberal and exceedingly straightforward individual, who, alas, was assassinated in after years when the savage military group took power in Japan. Perhaps of even greater interest to me were my meetings with some of the political leaders of the country, especially the Elder Statesmen, who, although they kept pretty well in the background, were accorded a veneration far exceeding that given, for example, to a worthy retired American President. It was arranged that I should meet several leading members of the Cabinet and of the Diplomatic Advisory Council; and finally Premier Hara himself gave me assurances that he desired the Japanese Group to enter the Consortium on the American plan.

Our daily discussions were interspersed with many entertainments, some of them purely social and others of the variety that bankers' associations and chambers of commerce always proffer the foreign visitor. In my wife's diary of those days is a description of one of the social occasions. She had been describing the rather feudal life that some of the noble families led in Japan;

and was speaking of a luncheon given for us by Baron and Baroness Iwasaki whose twenty-five acre estate was in the very middle of Tokyo where, for tax purposes, it was declared as "moor and forest land." My wife's brief description runs on:

March 11 — Thursday

This was the day of the great Iwasaki luncheon. I sat at Baron Iwasaki's right. He was a very large, very fat man. I found him rather fascinating. He was interested in music — asked all about the opera in New York. I told him about the Russian ballet, which he had never seen. He is much interested in the theatre, and has read a lot of Shaw and Oscar Wilde. He laughed at my impressions of the Japanese theatre, and agreed with what I said.

After luncheon we looked at the porcelain collection, and then went for a walk through the beautiful garden, one of the most famous in all Japan. Wild ducks were flying overhead, and some fishermen in a boat were casting a huge circular net — really a wonderful stunt, a little like throwing a lassoo. We walked over lovely stone bridges, and sometimes over the water on flat stepping stones. The stones were a great feature of the garden. They were of different colors and sizes, and had been placed with the utmost care. These stones had been transported all the way from Nagasaki. We wandered through the garden, which is built around a series of lakes. The water comes in from the bay and of course is salt. At last we came to their Japanese house (we had had luncheon in a European house) and were taken all through it. It was the first Japanese house I had seen and I was much charmed by it. It seemed to wander on endlessly, and was built around a series of little courts, so quiet, so secluded, such a lovely study in grey and green, the grey stones and gravelled walks, and the green pine trees. It would be a most charming place to spend a honeymoon. There were different kakemonas and pieces of porcelain and flowers in the kakemonas.

We then walked to a little tea house on the lake, where tea and cake and candy were waiting for us. Of course we were

233

starving, as we had only finished a three-hour luncheon half an hour before! Baron I. and I reached there first. He asked me if I would like a cigarette, and I said I should if it was all right for me to smoke there and if it would not be displeasing to the Baroness. He said not at all, as the Baroness herself liked to smoke. So I took a cigarette, and when the Baroness came, the Baron, her nephew (the Baroness was quite old), offered her a cigarette. She refused with considerable astonishment and emphasis. Then the Baron said some of the crossest and sternest Japanese words that I had ever heard, and the Baroness took the cigarette with alacrity. I am sure that she had never touched one before, and the poor old lady's attempts to smoke it roused all my sympathy. Men are tyrants the world over!

Short weekend trips about the country had also been arranged, including one to beautiful old Kyoto, the ancient capital of Japan. The first morning we were there my wife, whose room in the hotel suite had a different outlook from mine onto the charming park that surrounded the hotel, complained that she had been kept awake by the noise of some animal under her window — "sounded just like a lion roaring," she remarked.

I at once said we would go to see the manager. Playing the part of a perfect husband, I explained to him tactfully that my wife was rather nervous and perhaps too readily overwrought, as she had the fantastic idea that she "had heard the roaring of a lion under her window."

"Oh, please, Mr. Lamont and Madame," wailed the manager, "so sorry, please excuse. Please, Madame, we do have pet lion. So sorry. Friend in Burma send me cub, but it grow so fast, please. So sorry. Will lock up lion in cellar, please."

One day we were taken to some of the old Buddhist

temples halfway up the hill back of Kyoto, with a superb
view of the surrounding mountains. Their old grey walls
were peeping from behind white and pink blossomed
plum trees, with a background of dark pines, lofty and
spreading, the branches growing out horizontally, as one
always sees them in the Japanese pictures. Further up the
high hill we went to one large and nobly proportioned
temple, beautifully decorated with black and gold lac-
quer, in which temple people were worshipping and
praying.

Then came another temple, higher up, and a quiet,
green spot, enclosed in a stone fence, with the steep
hill back of it where the ashes of believers were being
brought to be mingled with the ashes of the founder of
the sect. It was a rather touching ceremony. The nearest
relative of the dead man would approach the gate and
hand a simple wooden box filled with ashes to the priest
who stood at the gate. This priest handed it to another
priest, who walked slowly to the back of the enclosure,
where he deposited the ashes in a big stone basin. Then
the relatives withdrew to a small covered pavilion and
fell on their knees, while the priests chanted the service.
There were no agonizing moments. The ceremony was
simple and dignified, and symbolic of the union of the
soul of the believer with the souls of other loved ones.

We were a month in Tokyo. At the end of that time
Governor Inouye told me that the Japanese would, as to
those two Chinese provinces, waive all special claims of
a permanent character, but that there were two or three
minor operations, short railway spurs, in Manchuria
and Mongolia, not having to do with the central Chinese

Government, that the Japanese had started and must complete. The so-called military element had carried on a steady opposition to withdrawal of the reservations, on the ground that the Western nations would, under American leadership, endanger Japan's general interests in Manchuria. Thus the withdrawal in principle, with the seemingly minor reservations attached, seemed about as satisfactory as could be expected. Japan, be it remembered, already controlled the main railway line that ran from North to South Manchuria.

I told the Governor that the proposal seemed fairly satisfactory, but that I must communicate with the Western Governments and their Groups for their views; that meantime I would take my projected trip to China to try to find out what it was we were all talking about, would spend April there and would stop back in Japan a week for the round-up. The only objection that the Japanese had to this schedule was that I should miss cherry-blossom time in Japan.

24

ACROSS THE CHINA SEA

We embarked for China at Kobe, after a rail ride along the shore of Japan's lovely Inland Sea. After a none too comfortable five-day steamer trip on the China Sea we landed in the clatter and turmoil of Shanghai. Shanghai has been variously characterized in novels and otherwise as the wickedest city in the world. Certainly, even a quarter century ago, it was cosmopolitan enough. People of every hue and race thronged its streets, and after nightfall I have no doubt it would have been equally easy to engage either a ricksha or a dagger-man. The Bund along the harbor was broad and crowded day and night, and the babel of tongues was deafening at all times.

I had avoided any measures of publicity. Yet our arrival was greeted with an uproar both of welcome and criticism, and there were scores of individuals and delegations, not to mention the newspaper men, impatient to see us. It did not take me long to wake up to the situation and to find there was strong influence being urged against the functioning of anything to do with the Consortium. I was deluged with anti-Consortium memorials, and protests from groups and individuals, laboring under the mistaken idea that I had come out for the purpose of imposing a loan on the Chinese Government. Where did all this hue and cry come from?

It was inspired, I learned, largely by the same Japanese military element that at Tokyo had so stubbornly clung to the reservations as to Japanese cooperation in the Consortium. They were using units of the Chinese vernacular press, owned by certain Japanese, and they extended their opposition through many other channels above- and under-ground. Beyond all, however, was the strong feeling that the Peking Government could not be trusted to carry out any serious obligations, and that it should not be bolstered up in any way.

I had barely settled down in my hotel before word came that a large group of students was gathering before the entrance, as a protest, prepared, some said, to stone our windows and very possibly ourselves. However, representatives of the Student Movement Association, introduced by George Sokolsky, an American, came in at my invitation to have tea with me. I had never met a keener, more eager, intelligent group of young men and women. They were strongly opposed to their own administration, very critical of the Japanese whom they accused of seeking to debauch and destroy their Government, and generally fearful of foreign domination.

It took a two-hour talk to get things fairly straightened out, and to convince the students that the Consortium would never undertake any operation unless it were constructive and unless the Chinese people themselves, by expression through their Government, showed that they wanted it. But the student body, which had con-

siderable power as a political group, was deeply dis-
trustful of Japan and of everything connected with the
Government of that country. The students were in fact
attempting to establish a boycott of Japanese goods.
Their gesture vis-a-vis the Consortium caused concern in
government circles at Peking, and various students that
had been imprisoned for revolt were suddenly released.
There was, however, one factor that was constantly
favorable to America. That was the action of our Government, following the serious rebellion of 1901, in devoting its share of the Boxer indemnity to the education
of Chinese students.

The whole political situation was far worse than I had
realized when I had talked with President Wilson at
Washington before my departure. Two rival governments were struggling to exert authority — the leading
one at Peking, where the revolution of 1911 had found
expression in a so-called republic that nominally took
over most of the rickety functions of the old Manchu
dynasty. It had at least some of the panoply and trap-
pings of the old Manchu Dowager Empress, who in her
latter days must have had a short temper. For she was
the centerpiece of the old story that when her hair
dresser found and unhappily showed to her a single grey
hair in her head, she was so incensed that she had his
head cut off. I met one of her ladies-in-waiting who had
survived to marry an American — the Princess Derling
she called herself. She was, I must say, full of intriguing
reminiscence.

The other government, the Southern one, was led by
Dr. Sun Yat Sen who had managed to attain the title

"Father of his Country." He had married into the powerful Soong family, his wife being the elder sister of Mme. Chiang Kai-shek, of Mme. H. H. Kung and of T. V. Soong. In my first few days at Shanghai the local celebrities had arranged for me all sorts of hospitalities — tiffins and dinners, crowded with Chinese and foreign bankers, business men and others. These occasions naturally gave me an excellent opportunity to explain in little words for little fingers the simple objects of my mission: to meet face to face the great Chinese people; to explain the favorable disposition that the Americans and other foreign banking groups had towards China and their desire to help it in some of its economic difficulties, due to lack of transportation, of adequate public utilities, and so on; to make clear that any advancement in the good-will purposes of the Consortium must certainly depend upon the wishes of the Chinese themselves.

At the end of a week, perhaps as a result of all these gatherings and of my scores of talks with important individuals, including leading journalists, there was a distinct let-up in the initial propaganda that had been so strongly directed against us. T'ang Shao-yi, an ex-Premier of China, a Liberal, by the way, who some years ago was supplanted in office by one of the militarists, put it to me this way:

"Since the outbreak of the Great War, especially in the year 1917, China has borrowed no less than two hundred and fifty million dollars silver from Japan. What has been done with this vast sum of money? Absolutely nothing! And where has the money gone to? Mostly into the pockets of some militarists and of those individuals who are now shouting against the new Consortium.

"These men have developed an appetite for Japanese money and are looking for more. When they hear, as they do, that the new Consortium will lend money only for constructive purposes and, moreover, will insist upon the money being spent for such purposes, they naturally oppose the Consortium from the bottom of their hearts. These men are being backed by a certain element in Japan. Thus they are enabled to buy up newspapers and start propaganda in opposition to the new Consortium, but not for a moment do they really represent our Chinese public opinion."

It was just about at this moment that I received from Dr. Sun Yat Sen a letter inviting me to pay him a call at his suburban villa. He explained — not altogether to my wife's satisfaction — that if he joined the others who had called on me in Shanghai, he feared that one of his enemies might bomb him, whereas he contemplated that no such attempt would be made at his own house.

The police said they would send me an escort, so I spent an afternoon with Dr. Sun. He explained to me afresh the calamitous division between North and South China of which I have spoken. He stated that the Southern faction which he headed was the one group in China that represented true-blue democracy, even though I could see no signs of it anywhere, but only evidences of confused and corrupt administration.

"President Wilson asked me," I remarked, "to find out whether there was any way to bring peace between the South and North so that, joined together, the two governments could make proper disposition of the Tuchuns, or War Lords, that ravage and bleed the intervening country and leave all China in turmoil."

"Peace between the South and North?" repeated Dr. Sun crisply. "Why yes. Just you give me $25,000,000, Mr. Lamont, and I'll equip a couple of army corps. Then we'll have peace in short order."

This, from one supposed to be China's great exponent of peaceful leadership and of democratic processes in place of military ones, would, I decided, be a bit disappointing to President Wilson.

Having gained in my Shanghai visit about all the information that I could about South China and having formed many useful contacts, I decided to turn north and take train for Peking. Meanwhile I had become somewhat annoyed by the assiduous presence of a couple of Japanese spies. Installed, as they arranged to be, in rooms on both sides of my secretary's room, which I used as my office, they made no glaring attempts at espionage. Yet merely to have them around was a nuisance. They were very clumsy. John Marquand's "Mr. Moto" was Machiavelli compared to them. I had with me no valuable documents save the cable code-book of the Morgan banking firm, and although I thought it an unnecessary precaution, my secretary always took it to bed with him and insisted upon sleeping with a loaded revolver under his pillow.

I had made no secret sorties, had held no surreptitious visits, in fact I had encouraged my secretary to make known my daily schedule. My annoyance was finally tempered with a little pity, for I could imagine what dull reading these espionage reports to the Japanese Home

Office must have been. But there the two little spies were, and there they stayed. Their attention was really a compliment to me and during my stay in the Far East it was a never-ceasing one: on the train to Peking, at the Grand Hotel there for three weeks, then again on the journey north to Mukden, through Manchuria and Korea and back to Tokyo. The personnel of my attendants was changed now and then, but all Japanese spies looked alike to me.

The railway cars were not like ours. The seats ran on either side up and down the length of the car, as in our old trolley cars. My secretary one afternoon brought to me a draft cable that I had just dictated. One of our little Jap friends became at once almost frenziedly interested, and across the car from us twisted his neck in an agonizing effort to glimpse the text of my cable. Whereupon (my wife testifies) I said to him in English quite pleasantly, "If you will come across the aisle and sit down by us you will have a much better chance to read this." The poor little chap gave a gasp and fell back, and one of our party more versed in Japanese folk-lore than I censured me, saying I had made the poor spy lose face completely, and very possibly he might go home and commit hara-kari.

Afterwards I asked one of the Japanese Government people what the idea was in trailing me all those weeks through China. He apologized, explained that it was one of those unfortunate routine practices that the Secret Service, leading its own existence independent of the general Government, always followed. He begged me not to mention it again, saying that Premier Hara, who,

243

I must say, had been most kind to me, would be infinitely embarrassed.

25

PEKING AND NORTHERN CHINA

We arrived at Peking in the dusty glare of a late April day. What is the most beautiful city in the world? Paris, Florence, Rome, Vienna, London, New York? Peking surpasses them all, in a way that I cannot attempt to define. Its loveliness does not rest chiefly in its temples, though the Temple of Heaven in form and coloring is bewildering in its beauty. Does it lie in the Forbidden City, that magnificent cradle of the ancient Manchu dynasties? Or in the old crooked streets that at almost every turn may disclose the walls of a lovely palace that lies hidden and mysterious within? Or does the charm come from the night sounds of the city, the dull tolling of the bells in the Buddhist temples, or in the subdued chatter of the rickshaw boys playing at fan-tan below? Do they never sleep?

As the past-midnight strikes, and the busy hum sinks to a murmur, one can almost hear the whispers of the women in the summer palace, the women surrounding the little boy Emperor, that boy who will never rule again. One senses the slow, deep breathing of millions of human beings that you almost hear about you, and that gives pulse and life and mystery to a great people.

Perhaps it is the element of surprise that is so stimulating and wonderful. You never know what is going to happen next. One's rickshaw boys draw up into a shop entrance to avoid the block close at hand. You peer ahead and see a smart motor car mixed up with a train of camels in the street, and the rickshaws and Peking carts having a collision. A moment later all the coolies may be shouting to each other to make way for the gay red and green funeral procession, while in the background rises the old red Chinese wall and a heavenly blue and green and red pagoda stands guard over the whole scene.

No group of people on this earth are to be so much admired, so pitied, so blamed for their virtues and charms and appalling shortcomings as the Chinese. They are the most fascinating and the most frustrating people in the world. With high intelligence, with minds filled with philosophy, poetry and a sense of beauty and color beyond compare, the Chinese have never become a nation. Having all the aspirations and all the catch-words and phrases of self-government and democracy, they yet lack the sense of administration and civic integrity. Corruption is decried by those of high and low degree, yet almost invariably practiced, and with shamelessness at that. The family being the unit of life, all members of the clan must see to it that their callings in life, official or otherwise, contribute adequately to the support of the clan. If a member of the family chance to be high in the civil service, it is his bounden duty to "squeeze" enough from his office to see to it that the family line flourish.

After I had spent only a short time in China, and especially after I had left the abominably cosmopolitan Shanghai, I had become entranced with the Chinese. Their mentalities and personal charm swept me off my feet. How could such a people, I asked myself, now that the ancient monarchy with its embedded traditions had fallen away, fail to be unmoved by the fresh breezes of freedom? Integrity and democracy in public service *must* now be the rule for this great people. I was thrilled with the future that I felt to be in store for this mass of 400,000,000 human beings.

I know I have just been writing a speech — expressing what I felt on that visit twenty-seven years ago and, too, what I said constantly to my own fellow-Americans, in many private and public addresses after my return home. In fact, I talked so much and with so much enthusiasm that before long I began to be classed as an "Expert on China," the sort of title that our communities here are apt to give to anyone who has spent a few weeks in the Far East and who, upon his return, is willing to tell far more than he knows.

We settled down very comfortably, our little mission and the two disconsolate Japanese spies, at the Grand Hotel de Peking. Then we began to be flooded with the same sort of attention that we had received at Shanghai. It was of a somewhat higher order, for Peking was not primarily a commercial town, but was the seat of such duly constituted government as there was, at that time. There were many highly educated individuals constantly to be met, Cabinet officers and otherwise.

First, however, we were to be honored with a special

247

performance by the most famous magician of North China. He was waiting after dinner at the foot of the grand staircase in the hotel. "Lon-tong, lon-tong, igu-lon-tong," he intoned again and again to call us to attention. Then he proceeded to favor us with his necromancy to an amazing degree. He seemed to have an endless supply of snakes, and pulled them with equal ease from his pockets, his mouth, nose and ears. Some of the tricks he had learned from the Indians, whence all Eastern wizardry is derived. He and some of his fellow craftsmen from Benares and Bombay must have had some working cartel arrangement. He had his orders to entertain us every evening when we were available — "Lon-tong, lon-tong, igu-lon-tong!"

Almost at once upon our arrival old President Hsu had sent his representative to call and invite us to luncheon at the presidential palace. President Hsu was a venerable and delightful mandarin who had the reputation of indulging every morning before breakfast in the composition of a poem. In the course of luncheon I said to him, "Mr. President, I hear considerable talk about the possibility of China turning Bolshevik."

"Oh, no, Mr. Lamont," he responded seriously. "China tried Bolshevism in the eighth and again in the eleventh century. It did not work. She will not try it again."

All this was through a very skillful interpreter. The Chinese are apt in language, as we all know. Just across the table sat the Minister of the Interior. At a pause in my conversation with President Hsu, the Minister leaned over to me and in perfect English said, "Can you tell me who is pitching for the Pittsburgh Pirates this year?"

It seems he had in his earlier years attended one of the technical institutes in Pittsburgh.

President Hsu had heard that my mission in China was partly to ascertain whether the Chinese Government was a good risk for a moderate railway construction loan, if a group of European and American bankers (the Consortium) were disposed to consider such an operation. The kindly President Hsu, having misgivings (all too justified!) as to the attractiveness of his Government as an obligor, remarked as we sipped our tiny cups of tea, that if I found myself unable to make a loan to his Government, he himself "would be willing to borrow $5,000,000 from me!"

As we met the various Government officials, it was only too evident that they were anxious for the Consortium to function, and especially for the American Group to have an important place in its deliberations and operations. They warmly welcomed my suggestion that the American Group, and other national Groups as well, each send a representative to live in Peking and keep close contact with the Government's currency and fiscal problems. Such a move would be added recognition of the Northern republic as contrasted with the Southern.

The matter of the currency was indeed a pressing one. In the course of World War I the Government had unwisely borrowed very heavily from the Japanese Government. How much of the amount was ever utilized for proper Government purposes nobody knew. At any rate a post-war inflation was already in progress, and was becoming a dreadful plague to trade, both internal and external. China's currency, in the best of times, was uncertain and was now having rough going. It was evident that if the Consortium were to function, a currency stabilization loan must be one of the first items on its agenda.

I had no especial job to accomplish in China, beyond first ascertaining the attitude of Government and people towards the Consortium, and next studying as much as I could current economic and political conditions, so that upon my return I might make an intelligent report to all the Groups in the Consortium. To both these ends our U. S. Legation people in Peking believed that continued contact with as many of the outstanding public officials and the community leaders as possible was important. From our Legation people themselves I had the utmost cooperation. Our Minister was absent, but the Secretaries, having received advance word from Washington, were extraordinarily attentive and useful. If in those days I had not been a hardy soul, I should have been overwhelmed by the mountain of entertainment and conference under which I staggered. Both the British and French Ministers were almost equally interested.

Meanwhile the women of my party decided to have a look at some of the antique and silk shops and bazaars that were part of modern Peking's repute. We were at first somewhat disappointed: the rather reserved shopkeepers seemed to display only ordinary stuff that one could always pick up in London, and at times even in New York. When I expressed to one of my Chinese friends my surprise at the shopkeepers' seeming apathy, he explained that unless prospective customers had been introduced and properly vouched for, the best shops never disclosed the choicest things they had in stock. Apparently, the word was promptly passed along; for every morning from that time on half a dozen local merchants led their donkeys, burdened with tempting treasure, into the hotel courtyard, there to unload and unroll for us great packs of silks and furs and rugs. And the shops suddenly became equally solicitous that we should see the best of their jewelry, jade and porcelain.

One morning upon my return from a conference my wife met me, greatly excited over two jade necklaces that she had discovered. She dragged me around to the shop and we were duly ushered into its secret recesses.

"There," my wife said, as the complacent old Chinese spread the necklaces for me to see, "there! I have told him I would take them, but that *you* would do the bargaining!"

I could almost have sworn that the sly old boy gave me a half-wink. At any rate, the jade was lovely and precious. So was the price. Perhaps that evening the old man was explaining at home how the wives of these strange "Melican" men were lovely, but untutored in the art of trading.

Another feature of our stay in Peking was our meeting with about thirty missionaries, medical and religious. From my boyhood days I had listened to my father's annual missionary sermon from the pulpit, followed by a special collection for the support of these intrepid explorers. Now, here they were, in the flesh. I had been asked whether I were willing to meet them. I was only too glad and honored. They came from far and near and we talked together for the better part of an afternoon. Some of their friends and associates had perished, slaughtered in the Boxer Rebellion, a score of years before. But all those memories they had put behind them. Their work, as they described it, was thrilling. It was constructive and educational, without cant and without attempt to bog down their effort with too much religious dogma.

This simple self-sacrificing group told me of the famine that was already gripping a good part of North China, due to repeated crop failures and to lack of east-west transportation facilities to reach the worst afflicted regions. I met no Chinese of high standing who failed to speak with appreciation and gratitude of what the American missionaries were doing for their people; and, too, the whole community was deeply grateful for the erection by the Rockefeller Foundation of the magnificent medical school and hospital in the heart of Peking. I like to think that upon my return home I had some influence in persuading John D. Rockefeller, Jr., and his wife to visit Peking and see for themselves what their immense benefaction had created for the Chinese.

Our Secretary of Legation at the time of my visit, Ray Atherton, very kindly arranged for us two or three weekend journeys into the country. One, for the men only of our party, was to the Western Hills, a region of myth and mystery and still infested with bandits that at times showed hardly the consideration that they should for foreign visitors. We made our journey on little Mongolian ponies, very swift and rather unsure of foot in the pitted and rocky roads that we followed at such a fast pace. Attendants brought along the food on donkeys.

Our camping place for the night was the outer court of an ancient temple where priests still chanted their rituals. A glorious sunset lighted the skies beyond the farthest of the Western Hills into which we had penetrated, and then darkness came down like thunder across the vast and rolling plain. The fires were lighted, the sentinels were posted, and after supper we sat around the blaze and listened to the recital of the native legends that had come down through the centuries. For all that we knew, we might be on the fringe of the region where homo sapiens—earlier than the Neanderthal man—first emerged from the misty past.

Then we were off to bed, but for me not to fall into a dreamless slumber. Every half hour or so I could hear the muffled tolling of a bell, and then a silvery tinkle coming from that part of the temple that lay across the courtyard. Finally I could stand the eerie blend of silence and sound no longer. I slipped from my pallet, and in my pajamas and slippers crept across the courtyard and stole into the temple. There up back of the altars, in midnight quiet, strode slowly and quietly back and forth three Buddhist priests, two of them chanting the rituals in low tones, the other noiselessly swinging some sort of vessel with fragrant incense. For a full half-hour I leaned against a pillar, finally becoming almost an acolyte in the mysticism of worship, feeling that overwhelming sense that comes from the darkness and mystery of a vast old world, whose beginnings had swung through the centuries long before our remote ancestors had ever crossed the Eastern and Western oceans.

253

Later there was another pilgrimage — this one to the
Great Wall. We were carried there in a small special
train. Up well to the north of Peking, not far from
Kalgan, we struck the Wall. Winding like a great and
impassive serpent for hundreds of miles up and down
over the countryside, hill, dale and mountain, the mas-
siveness and permanence of the Great Wall were what
struck us most. Broken as it was, and by "Time's fell
hand defaced," it stretched far to the west in immense
coils into Mongolia itself. To the east it kept on until
with a sudden turn it came down to the China Sea.
Through a breach in the Wall where we reached it there
was slowly stalking a caravan train of camels laden with
furs and rugs, hailing from I know not where beyond the
wild Mongolian country, but, as always, following the
ancient route of the caravans, and for part of the distance, of Marco Polo himself. This was the China of
the ancient of days, ever changing, yet ever the same.

There the Great Wall was, that barrier erected by an
early and highly cultivated Chinese civilization to keep
out the invading Tartar barbarians and the Manchus
from the north. The immediate purpose of the Wall, to
hold out the invaders, had failed, but the Chinese had
their revenge, for when after many years the barbarians
had stormed and breached the Wall, and made themselves conquerors of the promised land, the vanquished
nation had turned around and within a few generations
quietly absorbed the aggressors into their own race. Save
for the name of the Manchu dynasty, the barbarians
from the north and west had become a part of the ancient civilization of China.

The invaders had, however, brought into the promised land a strain of physique more robust though not more enduring than the conquered. I remember in 1917, during World War I, seeing in France thousands upon thousands of Mongolian laborers, brought over the stormy seas to work for the Allies — a magnificent set of men, tall, straight, strong and ruddy-hued — a type far different from that of the "heathen Chinee."

Until I inspected the Great Wall close at hand, its bastions and its crumbling turrets, I had not realized that every part of it was built of brick, and that those millions of brick had been lime-kilned and baked with wood fires. To procure that wood the Chinese had deforested their entire country within hundreds of miles of the Wall. That complete denuding of the landscape, that total destruction of the forests, had resulted in the terrible floods that for centuries have marked the great Chinese rivers, the Yang-tze, the Hwang-ho, the Si-kiang and others, that have swept away the crops season after season, and have brought to China that almost yearly famine that has ravished the country-folk and kept them half-starved.

Of course, there is much of China to which these remarks do not apply, but how can we expect a people over such vast areas as the great rivers drain to endure semi-starvation and at the same time to become a well-knit nation? On our return to Japan, we had to traverse Korea and there, although the Japanese had arbitrarily installed themselves only ten years before, the hillsides and sterile plains were already alive with active reforestation. From the train the young trees, set out to conserve the land, looked like growing crops. But in a few years

255

more they would be full grown. The Japanese were too wise to allow the destruction of forest reserves to continue, as had the Koreans and Chinese.

26

FAR EAST MISSION COMPLETED

My counsel, Jeremiah Smith, had left us to return to Tokyo a few days in advance, and, with Governor Inouye of the Bank of Japan, to put into legal shape for signing, the reservations agreed upon by the Japanese Group as to their concessions in Manchuria and Mongolia. When we arrived at Tokyo we found that Smith and our really eminent Ambassador, Roland S. Morris, had the papers all in readiness for us to sign. Thus we had accomplished at any rate the formal aim of our mission. That was to persuade the Japanese Group to withdraw all special claims to concessions in Manchuria and Mongolia, except as to the short railways already under construction near the South Manchurian Railway which they already controlled.

In the course of our long-drawn-out discussions that had kept us in Japan all through March, it had become obvious that there was a distinct cleavage between the Japanese liberal groups which then controlled the Government and desired to work closer with the Western Powers, and the military set whose aims had not been declared, but whose opposition to the Consortium had been made clearer to us through their underground propaganda in China, designed to array the Chinese against the proposed operations of the Consortium.

Ambassador Morris, however, felt assured that, despite the aggressiveness of the Japanese militarists in seizing Formosa twenty-five and Korea ten years before, the liberal elements in Japan were in fairly secure control; and, now that the policy of association in the International Consortium had been adopted, were likely to continue so. He urged that I should have a talk with Prince Yamagata, by far the most distinguished and most respected of the Elder Statesmen. It was he, even then an old man, who had planned Japan's strategy in the war against Russia in 1904-5, and it was he who backed up President Theodore Roosevelt's terms as finally laid down before the emissaries of the two countries at Portsmouth in 1904, one of the most constructive acts that Roosevelt ever performed in international affairs.

Prince Yamagata received me at his villa the day of my departure for home. He was upwards of eighty years old, but tall, straight as an arrow and with features like those of the ancient Japanese nobles. We talked pleasantly for an hour about the mission I was on and about international cooperation in general. He asked me about China, although, of course, he knew far more than I did.

At the close of the interview, in which the Prince impressed me more than any other individual I had met in the Far East, I asked him whether he would be willing to comment to me on Japanese-Chinese and Japanese-American relations. He stood in silence for a moment and then said: "Mr. Lamont, I have been a soldier and have commanded armies. I am supposed to think along lines of military organization and of necessary force. But I have been sitting out here in the Eastern World now for years on end. I have been watching wars and counter-wars. Japan's policy towards China must always be one of peaceful penetration in trade. If we ever try to conquer and rule China we are lost. The Chinese, even though completely lacking organization, are a greater people than the Japanese. Our fate, and any attempt at conquest, would be like that of the Manchus centuries ago. We should be swallowed up and lost.

"As for America, Mr. Lamont, war with America would be complete disaster for us. We might gain something initially. Finally we should come to humiliating defeat.

"My two axioms are: with China peace and trade; with America friendship, always friendship and commerce as well."

My time was up. I wonder what the Prince's comment would have been if I had reminded him of his activity in the war against China a quarter century before; or whether if the Prince had been living up to the time of Pearl Harbor it would have made any difference. At any rate, what the Prince had said to me made the snow clad peak of Fujiyama take on an even rosier glow as we sailed out of Yokohama Harbor at the setting of the sun that day.

27

IN RETROSPECT

The journey home from the Far East was pleasanter than the trip outward bound. For one thing it was mid-May and the ocean was indeed pacific. The Chinese stewards in their long blue denim frocks were as solemn as ever — "blackbelly pie or lice pudding?" was their usual formula for dessert. The brief stay at Honolulu, greeted as old friends by the ever hospitable Dillinghams, the gorgeous bathing at Waikiki Beach, and the warm welcome at San Francisco by an assorted committee of bankers and leading citizens who staged for us a wonderful luncheon of two or three hundred people, all made the trip home a particularly enjoyable one. We stopped off at Chicago for the Republican Convention, and so it was July before we reached the East coast.

By early autumn the famine which threatened when I was still in Peking became a hideous reality. Word came that millions were starving, that all China turned its eyes to America for help. President Wilson at once asked me to act as chairman of a committee to make a drive for China Relief, and soon I found myself recounting to generous audiences the appalling features in the calamitous Chinese situation. Nothing at that time could daunt my confidence in a fine future for the Chinese people. I spoke with genuine admiration for them; and I remember how enthusiastically my words were received when I characterized the Chinese as "an industrious, intelligent, sober, peace-loving people, that I believed to be steadily forging ahead to become a strong, united nation." About $8,000,000 was contributed to the Fund.

As for the Consortium for the Assistance of China, we held in 1921 a full-dress meeting in New York, attended by delegates from all four national Groups, British, French, Japanese and American. We ratified the formulas I had reached with the Japanese Group in Tokyo, and in effect we declared ourselves prepared to do business. My report had made clear, however, my judgment that until the two Chinas, the South and the North, came together, until a new, national parliament stood ready to approve all operations, it would be unwise for the Consortium to undertake any fresh loans.

As the years rolled by, it became clear that neither the Chinese Government nor its provinces were in a position to command credit. Politics in China, instead of bettering, gradually worsened. The power of certain of the War Lords may have lessened, but there was no attempt at firm cohesion, and no unified political or economic structures upon which Consortium loans could be safely offered to Western investors.

The International Consortium had been established on sound principles. The governments sponsoring the four national Groups were gratified with the joint approach to Far Eastern affairs that had been arranged. They felt that already the meetings of the Consortium delegates had been fruitful in ironing out to a material degree the attitudes of the various powers towards China. They were extremely anxious for the political unification of China itself, and equally so for her economic development. Indeed, the individual representatives of the Groups resident in Peking for several years made every effort, gave every inducement, to get the Government started on a program of public improvements that would have meant to the Chinese infinite benefit in relief and in living standards. Yet nothing could be done to remove the dead hand that China's lethargy and corruption in politics laid upon real national progress.

The final quietus to the Consortium came when the New Deal in America reverted in effect to the original William Jennings Bryan attitude of 1913, by setting up on the statute books a law that prevented banks from underwriting or taking part in loan issues. That law led automatically to the dissolution of the American Group, of which the other Groups were duly notified. Following American action came the wind-up of the Consortium itself. This action was a heavy blow to the late Sir Charles Addis, of the Hongkong and Shanghai Banking Corporation, a noble soul who had spent many of the younger and middle years of his life in China, and who had the fondest hopes for the development of that country. In the years since 1919, I had, perhaps, travelled further afield and been more active in the affairs of the Consortium, but Sir Charles Addis had in reality been the heart of the enterprise.

At least the Consortium members had the sorry satisfaction of knowing that over the years they had, at the behest of their several governments, spent of their own money, without a penny of recourse, upwards of $900,000 in administration at home and in China, in cable tolls and other outlays. In conception and while it lasted, the Consortium was a "noble experiment" in international cooperation. Had its plans been possible of realization, the steady progress in cooperation of the national Groups — British, French, American, Japanese — on the mainland of Asia might well have proved the vital factor in restraining Japan from her outrageous breach of the Nine Power Pact by her invasion of Manchuria in 1931. That put an end forthwith to all hopes.

Finally as to China, for 150 years, since the days of the old clipper trading ships in the early nineteenth century, we Americans have felt and expressed a peculiar affinity for the Chinese people. We have admired their exceptional qualities; we have forgiven their failings. Successive administrations at Washington have been persistent in their efforts to bring about a closer relationship with China. About a hundred years ago we succeeded in establishing missionary centers and hospitals that proved of immense value to the Chinese, who long before had begun to regard America as their most sympathetic and helpful friend among the nations of the West. The signing of the Nine Power Pact at Washington in 1922 was another step forward, for by its terms the United States, Britain, France, Italy, Japan, China, Belgium, Holland, and Portugal pledged themselves to the principle of preserving the territorial and political integrity of China.

For a long time after my return to the United States,

I continued to descant upon the Chinese people, upon their virtues and upon the glowing future which I felt lay before them. In recent years, however, I have been one of the thousands of Americans who have been disappointed and begun to despair — I hope that is far too strong a word — over China's political and economic future. Contrary to all our expectations there has been no group powerful enough to establish stable government, untainted by corruption. Nor has anyone seemed to care about democracy.

So far as I can see, in no respect is the political situation of China better today than it was when I studied the country briefly a quarter century ago. Then there was the constant though undeclared war between North and South. Then the Tuchuns, the War Lords, dominated and sucked dry the intervening country. Now, as then, the question with the ruling regime is not first of all how to unify the disparate elements, but how to overwhelm the opposition with force.

On my visit it was Dr. Sun Yat Sen, the leader of high renown, who wanted $25,000,000 to equip an army and crush his opponents. Now it is his younger brother-in-law, Marshal Chiang, who asks for America to equip his rabble armies to the same end, in order to crush his opponents coming down from the North, the so-called Communist armies. Much as I detest Communism and the police state (which seems to be its outward and visible sign), I still believe that the Northern armies may be ranked as Chinese first and Communists second, and that in any event they are not to be won over merely by force of arms.

Today as in the past the opposing forces sway hither and thither over the countryside. And all the time the people of the land continue to suffer for lack of conservation improvements, agricultural machinery and all the equipment that might give them a chance for halfway normal existence. Further, the country continues in the throes of a currency inflation that is catastrophic.

But in China time is endless. A century with the Chinese people is but as a generation with us. No American can today predict China's future. It lies in the hidden mystery of years to come.

28

CONCLUSION

Meanwhile throughout that first decade following 1919, the American banking and investment community made great effort, with the approval, and not infrequently at the request, of the Washington Administration, to cooperate in the restoration of normal conditions in Europe. The necessity of stabilizing the leading currencies in order to stimulate trade once more was urgent, and under the leadership of J. P. Morgan & Co., American bankers and investors provided various credits and loans to foreign governments. My associates and I were active in most of these operations, and often it was my lot to be on the spot in Britain, France, or wherever at the time the loan plans were being worked out.

While conditions on the continent of Europe were badly upset, the distress and confusion in those days were not comparable to those prevailing today after World War II. Thus, with great organized effort, it was possible for the American banking and investment world to accomplish a task that today can be undertaken only through the cooperation of governments themselves. Twenty-five years ago a critical currency or exchange situation in one of the European states might be cured by a temporary American advance of $100,000,000. Today the corresponding essential sum might well run into a billion, or several billions of dollars.

Bad as were the economic and financial conditions in Europe following World War I, nevertheless they were sufficiently within control to be handled largely by private banking and investment interests. Today, two years after the end of World War II, the chaos in Europe is so complete that only strong governmental action can hope to reduce it to some degree of order. It should be noted also that now, just as in the years following World War I, what the European countries need as a prerequisite to restoration is the stablization of national currencies, so that normal trading can be resumed.

The result of the private banking operations a quarter century ago, was to stabilize Europe for a period of, say, ten years, and thus to enable her to get upon her feet. Indeed, until the rise of the dictators and their wilful disregard for the interests even of the countries that they ruled, the general feeling was that Europe was working back to economic conditions favoring a long period of peace.

My observation of the European chaos of today, following World War II, takes me back by way of comparison to the somewhat lesser suffering and turbulence that I witnessed at close range after World War I. More than ever before has it been brought home to me that American foreign policy must be guided by accurate and adequate information regarding international conditions; and must be based both upon our own self-interest and upon a humane understanding of the world's needs. That is the only chance of salvation for mankind.

INDEX

INDEX